The Horse's Muscles in Motion

Sara Wyche

The Crowood Press

First published in 2002 by
The Crowood Press Ltd
Ramsbury, Marlborough
Wiltshire SN8 2HR

British Library Cataloguing in Publication Data
A catalogue record for this book is available from the British Library.

ISBN 1 86126 456 9

Dedication
To Jim.

Acknowledgements
It goes without saying that any book on the subject of anatomy owes its inspiration to the living
model: in this case, the horse. However the author is particularly indebted to the inspiration
provided by certain special horses and, inseparably, their dedicated owners. Horses such as Mia,
Estoril, Lucy and Tom, My Liege and Girlie, ponies such as Fly, and the occasional donkey, who,
together with their owners – N. Kerslake, M. Brownell, R. Tyrrell. J. Beasley, M. Phillips – are
among the many who overturned poor prognoses by questioning the opinions of mainstream
veterinary medicine.

The work in this book complements the many discussions of joint mechanics and muscle
function that were begun over the stable door or over the telephone. It is gratefully
acknowledged that such a project would not have been possible without this dialogue.

A special word of thanks is due to Mrs Jean Hammond, principal of Tollers Design Centre,
who condensed the history of painting movement into a tea break and who, in the world's
shortest art lesson, managed to sort out the white from the black.

Line-drawings by Sara Wyche

Edited and designed by OutHouse Publishing Services,
Shalbourne, Marlborough, Wiltshire SN8 3QJ

Printed and bound in Great Britain by Bookcraft, Midsomer Norton

Contents ——————————————————

Author's Note

The author is not a trained artist and hopes that any faults in technique will be forgiven. Occasionally it has been necessary to elongate structures and widen apertures in order to reveal elements that would normally be hidden. Any small degree of 'artistic licence' will be noted on the appropriate page.

It should be said that under no circumstances does the book claim to make any new discoveries in the science of biomechanics. The anatomy of the horse (for example, skeletal conformation, ligament placement, origin and insertion of muscles) is well documented: this book simply presents anatomical fact from a new perspective. Therefore, although the full orchestration of movement has yet to be analysed, the standard anatomical tunes are freely available to all. In this case, they have been taken from the following textbooks:

Stashak, Ted S., *Adams' Lameness in Horses*, 4th edition, Lea & Feibiger, Philadelphia, 1976.

Nickel, Schummer, Seiferle, *Lehrbuch der Anatomie der Haustiere*, 4th edition, Verlag Paul Parey, Berlin and Hamburg, 1977.

If the reader should find discrepancies (for example, sites of muscle insertion) between this and other anatomy books, it is hoped that these inconsistencies will be negligible and not affect the picture as a whole.

Introduction

'Have you ever noticed the fact that children always ask "why", but adults invariably tell them "how"?' This observation was made by a dressage rider who had problems finding a satisfactory saddle. Consequently he took several saddles apart to discover how they were made, then, by asking the question why, set out to challenge the use of traditional materials and methods of construction. The result was a uniquely flexible saddle-tree that eliminated many of the pitfalls associated with conventional design.

When riders have problems with their horse's movements, they cannot, of course, physically dismember the horse. However, as long as the horse is sound, perhaps only the most inquisitive rider wants to know how. It's not until the horse goes lame that we all want to know why.

The examination of horses for lameness has always occupied a large part of the equine veterinary practice. It has done in the past and will probably do so well into the future. With the sophisticated techniques available in specialist clinics, it is now possible to diagnose diseased tissue, often with pinpoint accuracy. But whereas the discovery of acute trauma (for example, bone fracture or tendon rupture) immediately explains how the horse went lame, the diagnosis of chronic wear and tear (for example, degenerative spinal or joint disease) often fails to explain why.

There are many factors that contribute to degenerative processes in the horse's musculoskeletal system, but there can be no doubt that some are linked to the way in which the horse is ridden. Although nobody rides with the intention of constricting the horse's joints, compressing the ligaments, or compromising the muscles, the fact remains that chronic unsoundness can develop only when the horse's body is, in some way, repeatedly misdirected. Since it's not likely that the horse inflicts such unsoundness on himself (at least, not without good reason), we have to consider the possibility that degeneration is unwittingly caused by a rider's lack of awareness of simple relationships in the horse's anatomy.

The musculoskeletal system can be divided into two types of tissue: rigid and elastic. The rider directs the horse's movements through the elastic tissues (muscles, tendons and ligaments), which in turn direct the rigid tissues (bones) to move the body from place to place. If the system is to remain intact, the energy released into it must be distributed correctly. The source of this energy is in the horse's muscles.

Ideally, the rigid and elastic tissues should be equal partners in the business of producing movement. They combine their efforts in a sort of musculoskeletal 'co-operative', which protects everyone's investment of energy and pays dividends in the conservation of fuel. Nevertheless, muscles have the ultimate power. If they abuse it, or abdicate their responsibility, then unhealthy cracks develop in the musculoskeletal organization, and these threaten the whole fabric of movement.

Of course horses run on the forehand, of course they hollow their backs, of course they trot along with their noses stuck out in front of them and their hocks insufficiently engaged under their bodies. It may be considered unaesthetic, but these movements are well within the horse's natural repertoire. They are not inherently harmful. Movements become damaging to the horse only when they are either unfairly dominated by the weight of a rider, interrupted by the rider's aids, or forced by the rider against the natural conformation of the joints. If then, as riders, we choose to disregard, and even deliberately disconnect, certain coupling mechanisms essential to the survival of the horse's musculoskeletal system, we do so to its detriment.

To describe the movement of muscles using the printed page obviously has its limitations, especially when computer programs now do this with greater realism. Nevertheless, pen and paper have the advantage of fixing an image in the mind's eye. In this book, the purpose of line-drawings is to freeze movements at certain moments in time in order to high-light the effect of muscles on vulnerable parts of the horse's skeleton.

However, regardless of the means, it is only the hallmark of good teaching if eventually the teacher becomes redundant. It is hoped that by the time the reader reaches the final pages of this book, he will be able to go out to the stable, look at the living horse, and understand the parameters of movement – without recourse to a textbook or indeed a laptop.

If, in addition, the book furnishes students and therapists with an accessible compendium of anatomy, that will be a bonus. At the very least, this book looks at the role of the horse's muscles in movement and, for the adult – and the child – in every horseperson, attempts to answer *how* they work, *why* they work, and why sometimes (despite our best efforts) they don't.

1 Introducing Anatomy

The assessment of conformation is an essential part of breeding and training horses. The aim is to evaluate an individual's potential by taking stock of his strengths and weaknesses. In the first instance, judgement is based on the appearance of the horse's exterior – for example, the visible circumference of bone and the angles of the joints. This may seem akin to judging a book by its cover, but it is a practical application of anatomy and it undoubtedly results in winners.

Bones and joints are justifiably regarded as the foundation of a horse's performance, not least because their size and shape determines an animal's capacity to carry muscle. Nevertheless, this preoccupation with the horse's skeleton also permeates the conventional way of looking at lameness. Many lameness investigations confine themselves to the evidence of radiographic and ultrasonic images: in other words they give diagnostic priority to diseases that affect the immediate vicinity of ligaments, bones and joints.

Whether it is the result of the high profile of physiotherapists in sport, the growing popularity of alternative medicine, or the widespread use of scintigraphy in equine clinics, horse owners are now moving away from a traditionally regimented interpretation of lameness. There is a collective and spontaneous will in the horse world (which once could envisage only joint disease and tendon breakdown as a cause of lameness) to adopt a more holistic approach to the horse's locomotor system. Suddenly, at the top of everyone's agenda are muscles.

For example, if ever it could be said that riders, like the average car user, had very little notion of 'what goes on under the bonnet', that cannot be said today. Education in the relevance of anatomy for a new generation of saddle-fitters, and the continued popularity of dressage riding, are two factors responsible for the upsurge of interest in the role of the horse's muscles.

However, there are more than one hundred and fifty muscles in the horse's body, and it is not surprising that different professional groups emphasize those muscles that are most relevant to their areas of expertise. Unfortunately, this process has led to some muscles being given an importance that is not entirely deserved.

If horse owners should ever feel intimidated by anatomical one-upmanship (on the part of saddlers, trainers or even vets), they may rest assured that there are many more muscles that contribute to the horse's movement or his saddle fit than the much quoted 'trapezius' or 'longissimus'.

THE LANGUAGE OF THE BODY

All horse people are familiar with the term 'body language'. Whether or not we subscribe to current trends in natural horsemanship, body language is an essential part of communication in any branch of equestrianism. It comprises the sum total of conscious and subconscious gestures that enable humans and horses to participate in a 'conversation'. However, if it's the body that speaks the language then it's the muscles that supply the words.

Students of equine or veterinary science will probably agree that learning the anatomy of muscles is like jumping a cross-country course. The track is lengthy, often uphill, with a variety of imposing obstacles. For example, some muscles have names the size of tree-trunks and are therefore not for the faint-hearted. Some muscles form tricky combinations and cannot be taken individually. And some muscles are fixed to more than one point: understanding how these work depends on which route you take.

However, if there are hurdles in learning anatomy they are not very different from those encountered in learning a language. For example, in language we have to know how to arrange words correctly before we can grasp the meaning of a sentence . Similarly, we have to learn where to place muscles correctly in relation to the skeleton before we can understand what they mean in movement.

We could even think of the muscles as letters of an alphabet. Individually, muscles have no meaning. It is only when they work as a group that they produce a single movement – the equivalent of a word. When one muscle group links up with another group, they produce a pattern of movements – the equivalent of a phrase or sentence. Just as words can be combined to make sense, or even nonsense, so there are combinations of movements that make sense, and combinations (usually enforced) that make no sense at all.

If movement is language, then anatomy holds the key to its grammar. Knowing the position of muscles in relation to the skeleton is part of understanding that grammar. For any additional explanations, we can always consult a dictionary. Unfortunately, the dictionary of anatomy is written in Greek and Latin, which is a pity since clues to the skeletal whereabouts of muscles are often concealed in their names.

On the face of it, the lengthy and rather venerable names of muscles make for a fairly indigestible diet of words. It is true that 'biceps' and 'triceps' have found their way into the vernacular, 'pecs' are body-building jar-

gon, and 'cruciates' are what footballers regularly sacrifice on Saturday afternoons. But 'common digital extensor' is barely common parlance, brachiocephalicus' sounds like a dinosaur, and 'teres major' could be the key signature of a symphony. When it comes to 'vastus intermedius', 'latissimus dorsi', or 'rectus capitus', one might be forgiven for thinking these were heroes in a Roman epic!

The reason for the apparent inaccessibility of anatomy labels is that their origins lie in the history of medicine. In centuries gone by, without the provision of an internationally available computer database, each newly discovered muscle, tendon, nerve and ligament had to be described in a way that was intelligible the world over. Furthermore the names had to include connotations of shape, function or situation (and preferably all three), yet, at the same time, not be liable to misinterpretation. This meant that a common terminology was necessary, and this was automatically derived from the scholarly, classical languages of Greek and Latin.

Science still coins words from these languages, but because the words describe new technology, they melt unobtrusively into modern English.

A PLACE FOR EVERYTHING ...

Leornardo da Vinci did it. So did George Stubbs. In order to portray humans and horses in the most life-like way, they undertook to study anatomy. This did not mean going down to the local library; it meant collecting corpses, and taking them apart. Working from cadavers, these artists taught themselves the principles of anatomy by peeling back the layers of flesh and systematically drawing what they saw.

However, the difficulty in studying muscles by paring them away (dissecting them) is that you have to know what they do before you learn where they are. This may sound like a contradiction, but, for hundreds of years, that is how it has been.

Illustrators of anatomy textbooks have traditionally drawn muscles by starting at the body's surface and working down through the layers until they reach the skeleton. This imitates the method of dissection and is perfectly legitimate for producing diagrams intended to provide anatomical reference points for surgery. (For obvious reasons, this is how the surgeon reaches the operation site.)

Visually removing the muscles layer by layer is a way of showing how they are organized. Unfortunately, it is not a way of showing how they work. In most cases it is almost impossible simultaneously to illustrate the substance of a muscle and its points of attachment to the skeleton. Nevertheless, the location of these attachments (called muscle origin and insertion) is strategically important for producing movement. Therefore, in order to reveal the mechanical action of muscles, the approach to portraying anatomy has to be different.

Anatomical dissection could be compared to stripping an engine, with one significant difference: you can put the engine back together. The process of rebuilding a machine probably tells you more about its mechanical properties than the act of dismantling it. For this reason, it is easier to understand the mechanical action of muscles if you look at their anatomy in the reverse order from dissection: that is, starting with the muscles closest to the skeleton and working outwards.

... AND EVERYTHING IN ITS PLACE

To build a machine, an engineer is inevitably faced with the problem of how to arrange the moving parts. Obviously, they should not impinge on each other because that causes friction, but neither should they occupy too much space because that is likely to make them mechanically inefficient.

The moving components of any machine invariably require joints. Whether the machine is man-made, or made out of flesh and bone, the structure is governed by what the joints are expected to do: by the load they carry, the energy they transmit, and by their estimated range of movement. The chosen shape of a joint dictates its action. For example, a sphere can swivel round its entire circumference, whereas a cylinder rotates around a single axis, and a plane slides backwards and forwards. Therefore, once a joint has a given shape, its raison d'être is fixed for all time. To force it beyond its natural boundary simply results in unsoundness.

The joints of the horse are junctions between the moving components of a powerful, organic machine. They are made out of cartilage and bone, but they nevertheless have specific mechanical shapes and these rigorously define the parameters of movement. Muscles may converge on a joint from all directions, but this does not alter the fact that if a joint is designed to be a hinge then it is physically incapable of behaving like a ball and socket, and vice versa. Alternatively, if a joint has a potentially wide range of movement, it may rely heavily on muscles to protect it from injury.

The distinctive shapes of joints provide valuable clues to the mechanical possibilities of the muscles that move them. To overlook such clues is to miss the point about muscles. Muscles have to be understood in the context of their skeletal attachments and the joint structure, otherwise any attempt to describe their movement is meaningless.

Muscles, bones and joints are part of a living, mechanical jigsaw puzzle. Some of the pieces may appear to be frustratingly similar, but, of course, none of them are absolutely identical and all interlock in a most specific way. When it is finished, the puzzle will become a complete picture of movement. But, for this, the final piece has to be found, which, as in any good detective story, may not be until the very last page!

2 The Frame: Bones, Joints and Ligaments

Muscles and bones depend on the presence of the Earth's gravity. On the one hand, muscles use the force of gravity as a base line from which to measure the amount of effort needed to move the bones. On the other hand, gravity gives the bones weight, which enables them to act as a counterbalance to the power of the muscles. This interplay of muscle power and bone mass is crucial to the health of the whole musculoskeletal system.

Muscles and bones are therefore mutually dependent. Just as an engine needs a chassis, muscles need the skeletal frame to turn the power of movement into the reality of locomotion. Nevertheless, whereas the application of the body's muscles is physically ingenious, the structure of the skeleton is a mechanical tour de force.

You don't have to be a forensic scientist to recognize a bone. We all know the feel of bone and, if asked, we could probably draw an approximation of its shape, something between a cudgel and a dumb-bell. For people who breed horses, the word 'bone' is inevitably associated with feed rations of high protein, and mineral supplements containing calcium, magnesium and phosphorus. For those who advertise stallions, the term 'bone' may stand for that extra half-inch that adds value to the stud fee. People in every niche of equestrianism have a vested interest in the horse's bones, and, of course, size matters. However, in terms of overall construction, it is not enough just to have brute strength. There is far more to bones than that.

It may seem like a strange recommendation for horse owners, but a good way to learn about the implications of bone construction is by making a scale model. It requires only some modelling clay and yet – bearing in mind that the result is not supposed to be a work of art – it is a valuable lesson in mechanics. For example, we might think that to make something resembling the horse's cannon bone, we simply roll up a 'sausage' and then plump up the ends to look like joints. Nothing could be further from the truth.

Bones have features. They have protrusions, indentations and, in some cases, a degree of curve or twist along their axis. The extraordinary thing is that when making a replica of a bone out of soft material, the model refuses to keep its shape until the last feature is put in place. Indeed it continues to be obstinately bendy until the sum total of the dimensions is accurately balanced, when suddenly the structure becomes self-supporting. In other words, the ridges, grooves and protuberances of bones may appear to be external additions to the basic bone shape, but, like pillars and buttresses in architecture, they are an integral part of the construction. They have to be present before a bone is mechanically viable.

Making models may not have the authority of science, but the experiment serves to demonstrate that bones have built-in stability. It does not take a huge leap of the imagination to deduce that whenever a small amount of bony material is added or subtracted (as happens, for example, through injury or disease), there is a change in way the whole bone is loaded, and this consequently affects the balance of the muscles.

(It should not be forgotten that the central parts of many bones contain bone marrow. This means that, in particular, the core of long bones is not solid but tubular. However, if we consider the strength of man-made constructions using tubular materials – scaffolding for example – we can appreciate the probable load-bearing strength of the bones in the body's skeleton.)

Mechanically, therefore, each bone represents a complete structural package. In the fleet of bones that makes up the skeleton, there is no such thing as a basic model with optional extras. In fact, bones are rather like faces. By necessity they must have the skeletal equivalent of eyes, ears and noses, but these features can be assembled differently. It is this variation that gives the bones their individual identity.

In anatomy books, the illustrations of bones are like portraits. Of course, it goes without saying that they should be true likenesses. However, bones are moulded out of a single substance, and their surface features often lack sufficient detail to make them obvious. Because the contours are organic, and therefore uninterrupted, it is hard to identify them as parts of a precise mechanical tool. In other words, conventional pictures of bones are more like identikits. The images may be factually correct, but the presentation lacks depth, and the features mean something only to someone who knows them first hand. If the purpose of the illustration is to shed light on mechanical function then some other method of description has to be found.

In technical drawings of machines (for example, of car engines), it is easy to visualize the mechanics of movement because the components have well-defined geometric shapes. Whether they rotate, swivel, slide, or rock, depends on whether the parts are round, angular, spherical or cylindrical, spiral or plane. The action is in the geometry.

Imagine, therefore, that the musculoskeletal system is a living machine, and that the bones are mechanical components, bound by the same specifications as parts of any man-made machine. If we temporarily ignore the fact that they are living and focus only on movement, we can break down the bones into their constituent shapes, and replace each one with a simple geometric equivalent. It is a form of mechanical translation: substituting unembellished, but easily recognizable, geometric structures for the elaborate, living ones that are, unfortunately, rather vague. Of course, all translations lose something in the process, and, in this case, it will be the flowing lines of the original. However, by expressing these in a more straightforward way, the mechanics of movement become clear.

For example, consider the bones of the lower limb of the horse, the cannon bone and the two bones of the pastern. These have what might be described as a 'classic' bone shape: a straight, central shaft and bulbous ends. The joints between these bones (fetlock and pastern joints) all operate like hinges. However, there are subtle differences in construction, differences that have implications both for the horse's movement and for injury and disease.

By translating the shapes of the real bones into their, albeit imaginary, mechanical counterparts, with a central retaining feature in the fetlock joint but rounded outer edges in the pastern joint, it is clear that although the hinge mechanism is the same in all cases the structural security is not. Since the joints are held in alignment by strong, but nevertheless elastic, tissues (ligaments), it is evident that wherever the joint conformation is less the dependence on the ligaments must be more.

History shows us that there are countless ways to interpret the mechanics of movement, from puppets to mechanical dolls, from automata to robots. In the following pages, the interpretation of the horse's skeleton serves as a visual reminder of the mechanical stage upon which the horse's muscles play their part.

1. The bones of the horse's lower limb.

1. The cannon (or third metacarpal) bone.
2. The long pastern bone, or proximal phalanx.
3. The short pastern bone, or middle phalanx.
4. The pedal (or coffin) bone, or distal phalanx.
5. One of a pair of splint bones, or fourth metacarpal bone.
6. One of a pair of proximal sesamoid bones.
7. The navicular (or distal sesamoid) bone.

This anatomical picture will be familiar to most people. It illustrates the bones in three-quarter view, and it contains a good deal of visual information. For example, it shows us the relative proportions of the bones, the angles of the bones in relation to the ground when the horse is standing, and the location of certain surface bony features. However, although the image gives a greater sense of depth to the bones than when they are drawn in profile, it does little to help us understand the mechanical action of the joints.

As horse people, we are accustomed to handling the bones of the horse's lower limb when, for example, we pick out the feet or put on brushing boots. We know what the bones and tendons feel like, and we know their peripheral shape. But how can we equate our daily, manual experience with the technical information in this picture? Does it tell us what the joints do when we flex the leg? More importantly, does it make us aware of what the entire lower limb goes through every time the horse takes a step?

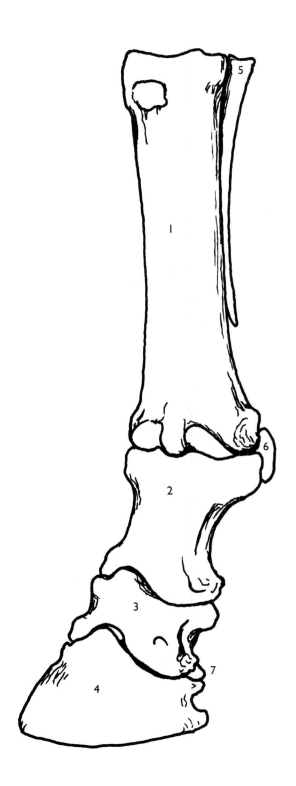

2. Translating the bones and joints into mechanical components.

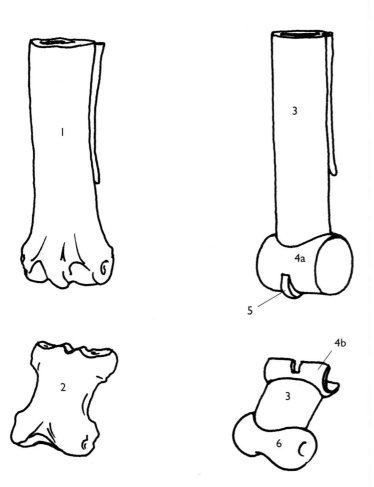

1. Cannon bone.
2. Long pastern bone.
3. Central rigid cylinder.
4. Fetlock joint:
   (a) joint surface of the cannon bone;
   (b) joint surface of the long pastern bone.
5. Interlocking key.
6. Pastern joint (one part only).

Conventional anatomical pictures of bones and joints may be life-like portraits but they do not convey a sense of movement. However, it is possible to break down the natural shape of the bones into constituent parts, and replace them with shapes taken from geometry. As a result, the images will no longer be direct representations of the living skeleton. In fact they will take on the appearance of parts of a machine. But because the 'robotic' bones are well defined, the mechanical action is less ambiguous. Furthermore, each mechanical shape will remind us of the specific movement of a joint once the muscles are superimposed.

For example, the cannon bone and the long pastern bone have 'classic' bone shape. Their central portions are rigid cylinders, and their joint surfaces combine to form a hinge mechanism. However, whereas the hinge of the fetlock joint is a straightforward barrel with a central interlocking key, the hinge of the pastern bone has a central dip and the barrel has rounded edges.

3. (A) The bones of the horse's lower limb. (B) An exploded mechanical diagram.

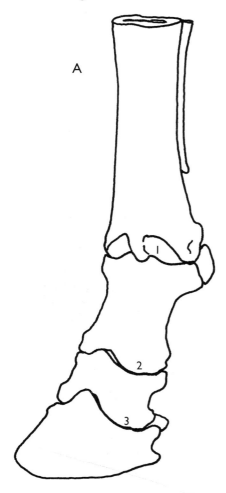

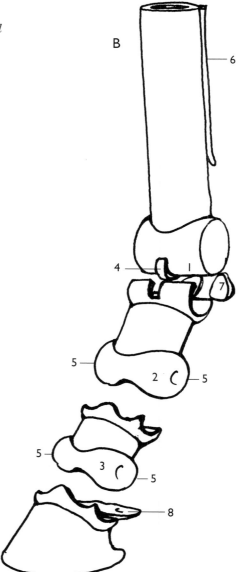

1. Fetlock joint.
2. Pastern joint.
3. Coffin joint.
4. Central key.
5. Rounded edges of both pastern joints.
6. Splint bone.
7. Proximal sesamoid bone.
8. Navicular (or distal sesamoid) bone.

The bones and joints have been given a mechanical 'make-over'. In each case, the joint movement is one of rotation around a single axis, like the hinge of a lid or a cat-flap. The variations in shape make it clear that whilst the two bones that make up the fetlock joint are locked in place by a central key, the bones of the pastern have the possibility of slipping from side to side. One splint bone, one proximal sesamoid bone, and the navicular bone are shown for anatomical reference.

4. The ligament system of the fetlock, pastern, and coffin joints.

1. Cannon bone.
2. Long pastern bone.
3. Short pastern bone.
4. Pedal (or coffin) bone.
5. Collateral cartilages.
6. Collateral ligaments of: (a) fetlock; (b) pastern; (c) coffin joints.
7. Ligaments of the proximal sesamoid bone.
8. Ligaments of the collateral cartilages.

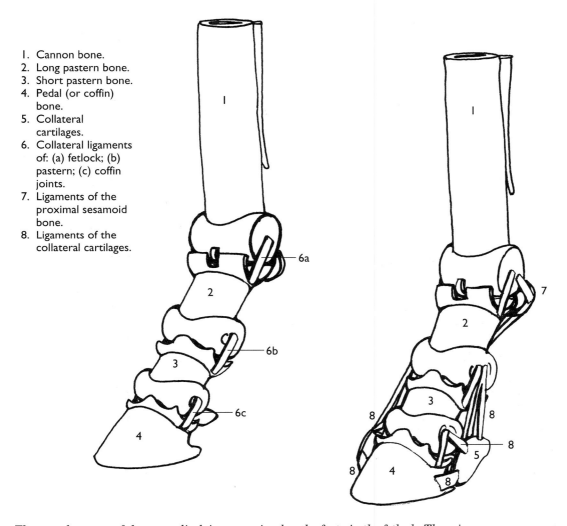

The muscle power of the upper limb is transmitted to the foot via the fetlock. There is a substantial change of direction in the angle of the bones at the fetlock, which means that this joint has to be tremendously stable. On the other hand, the pastern and coffin joints have to accommodate changes of surface in the ground.

Therefore, whereas it is in the fetlock joint's best interest not to move from sideways, it is a matter of basic self-preservation for both the joints below to move from side to side.

The lateral/medial (side-to-side) movement of the bones is restrained by soft-tissue structures called ligaments. A single ligament attaches to either side of each joint and holds the bones in alignment. Any identical structure found on both sides of a joint or limb is termed 'collateral'.

The conformation of the fetlock joint is complemented by two sesamoid bones. They are attached by ligaments to both sides of the cannon bone and to the rear of the long pastern bone. Ligaments connect the collateral cartilages to each of the bones of the foot.

5. *'Every step you take ...'*

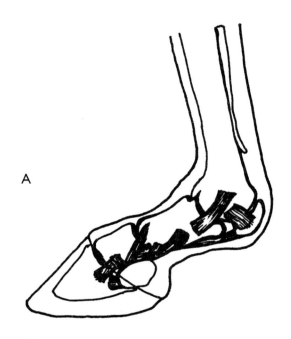

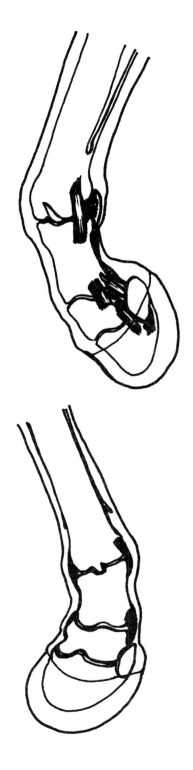

A. Loading the limb.
B. Making the transition from flexion
   to extension.
C. Tipping sideways.

*The principle direction of movement in the
fetlock, pastern, and coffin joints is backwards
and forwards. The only structures that stand
between the joints and their sideways
dislocation are the ligaments.*

6. Yet more ligaments.

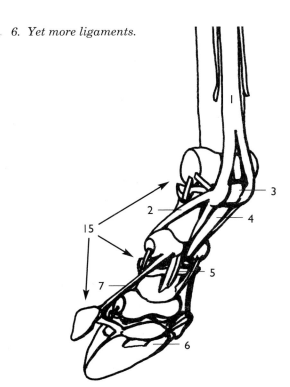

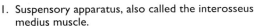

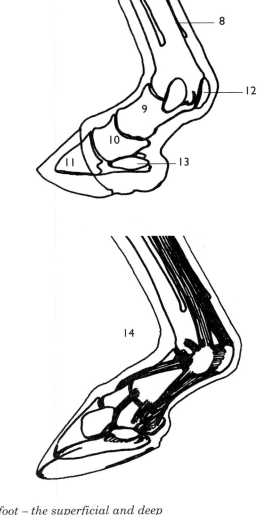

1. Suspensory apparatus, also called the interosseus medius muscle.
2. Extensor branch of the suspensory apparatus.
3. Intersesamoidean ligament.
4. Distal sesamoidean ligaments.
5. Palmar ligaments of the pastern joint.
6. Impar ligament of the navicular bone.
7. Collateral cartilage and navicular ligaments.
8. Cannon bone.
9. Long pastern bone.
10. Short pastern bone.
11. Pedal (or coffin) bone.
12. Proximal sesamoid bones.
13. Navicular (or distal sesamoid) bone.
14. Ligament support under the fetlock and foot.
15. The hinge principle of the fetlock, pastern, and coffin joints.

The major structures on the underside of the fetlock and foot – the superficial and deep digital flexor tendons – conceal an army of ligaments. The conformation of the fetlock is strengthened by the suspensory apparatus. This holds the proximal sesamoid bones in place and wraps itself around the long pastern bone to insert just above the pastern joint. The proximal sesamoid bones have ligament attachments to each other and to the long pastern bone. The underside of the pastern joint is quadruply supported. The distal sesamoid or navicular bone has a single ligament attached to the pedal (or coffin) bone, but is bound by collateral ligaments to the long pastern bone and the cartilages.

When the horse transfers his bodyweight from limb to limb, these ligaments prevent the hinges from being strained.

7. *The carpus, or 'knee'.*

1. Radius.
2. Proximal row of carpal bones.
3. Distal row of carpal bones.
4. Cannon (or third metacarpal) bone.
5. Accessory carpal bone.
6. Splint (or fourth metacarpal) bone.
7. A mechanical view of the double tier of hinges between (a) the radius and the proximal row of carpal bones, and (b) the proximal and distal carpal bones. The junction between the distal carpal bones and cannon bone is not part of this mechanism.
8. The carpal ligaments: (a) intercarpal ligaments; (b) collateral ligament; (c) ligaments of the accessory carpal bone to the radius, carpus and metacarpus.

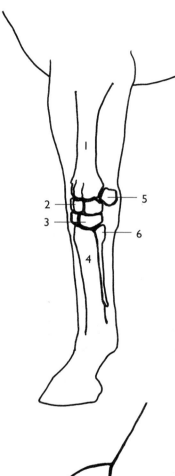

Although it is commonly referred to as a knee, this joint actually occupies the same place in the skeleton as the human wrist. Correctly called the carpus, the joint fulfils two functions. On the one hand it has to flex in order for the leg to be lifted from the ground. On the other hand it has to stabilize the entire forelimb while the body is propelled forwards. In other words, like the leg of a collapsible table, the horse's 'knee' can fold away or lock straight depending on the particular phase of movement.

The degree of flexion that allows the horse to tuck up his forelegs – not only to clear obstacles but also to curl up in his bed – is achieved with a double tier of hinges. As in the foot, collateral ligaments prevent the whole structure from deviating sideways, and intercarpal ligaments hold the small bones in their two distinct rows. The accessory carpal bone is an important place of insertion for muscles. It, too, is held in position at the carpus by ligaments.

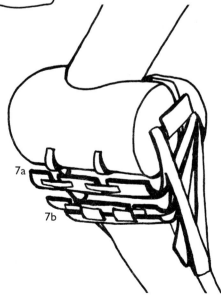

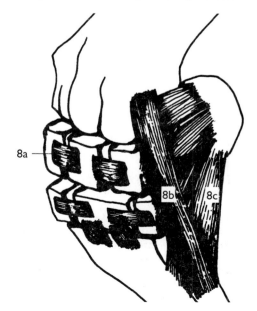

8. *The elbow joint.*

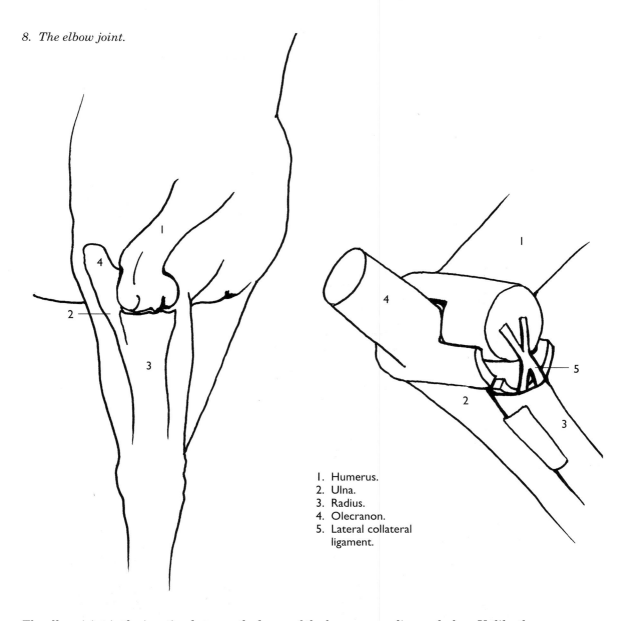

1. Humerus.
2. Ulna.
3. Radius.
4. Olecranon.
5. Lateral collateral
   ligament.

The elbow joint is the junction between the bones of the humerus, radius and ulna. Unlike the human radius and ulna, there is no rotation between these two bones in the horse. Instead the ulna is fused with the radius, and together the two bones form part of the, by now familiar, hinge mechanism with the end of the humerus.

The horse does, however, have a 'funny' bone. Called the olecranon, this is an extension of the ulna. From its lever-like shape and position at the rear of the joint, we can imagine that the olecranon has a significant role to play in mediating between the propelling power of the muscles above the elbow and the staying power of the muscles between this joint and the carpus.

The collateral ligaments are designed in such a way that, when the elbow joint is extended, they have a natural tendency to return the joint to its original position.

9. *The elbow joint: the underarm view.*

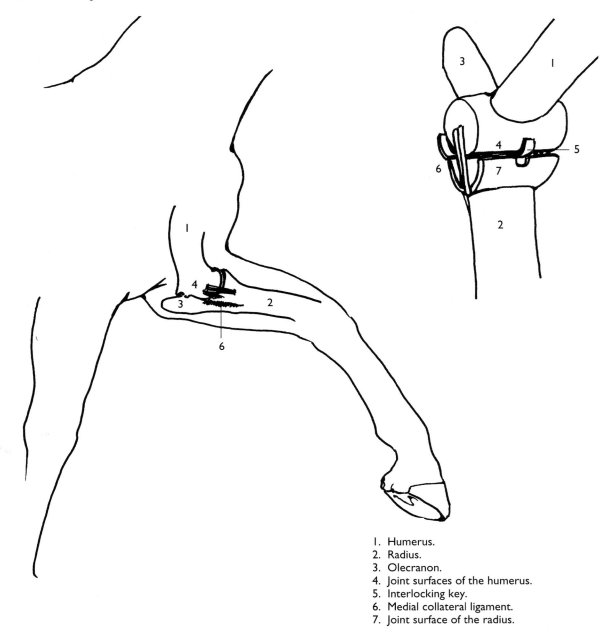

1. Humerus.
2. Radius.
3. Olecranon.
4. Joint surfaces of the humerus.
5. Interlocking key.
6. Medial collateral ligament.
7. Joint surface of the radius.

Although the structure of the elbow joint appears complex, it is, in fact, a basic hinge with a central interlocking key, not unlike that of the fetlock. The bones are more substantial and the joint surface is wider, but the principle is the same. The medial collateral ligament has a different configuration to its lateral counterpart, but it similarly helps to underpin the joint's movement by encouraging the hinge to 'snap' back into position.

10. Exposing the mechanics of the shoulder joint.

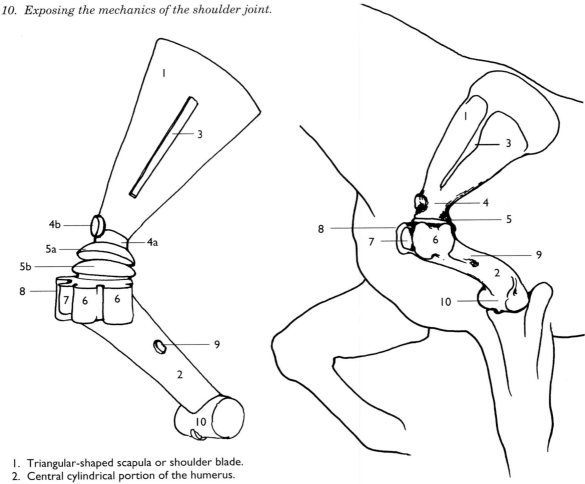

1. Triangular-shaped scapula or shoulder blade.
2. Central cylindrical portion of the humerus.
3. Spine of the scapula.
4. (a) narrow neck of the scapula;
   (b) supraglenoid tubercle.
5. Shoulder joint with: (a) socket; (b) ball surfaces.
6. Two eminences of the greater tubercle.
7. Intertuberal groove with intermediate tubercle.
8. Lesser tubercle.
9. Deltoid tuberosity.
10. Hinge mechanism of the elbow joint.

The shoulder joint is not a hinge, but an almost horizontal ball-and-socket. The 'ball' is formed by the head of the humerus. It is flat, and expansive. The 'socket' is contributed by the scapula, and does not cover the whole surface of the 'ball'.

The shoulder joint is unique because it has no ligaments of its own. The structures that determine the extent of movement all belong to the muscles. They simply double up as ligaments.

Compared to the narrow neck of the scapula, the top of the humerus is immensely strong and reinforced by bony features that protrude like buttresses around its circumference. Nevertheless, as it will be seen later, the shoulder joint is vulnerable and can be the source of a great deal of pain.

11. There are no joints connecting the bones of the horse's forelimb to the body.

1. Scapula.
2. Humerus.
3. Thoracic spine.
4. Ribs.

12. Interpreting the horse's pelvic girdle.

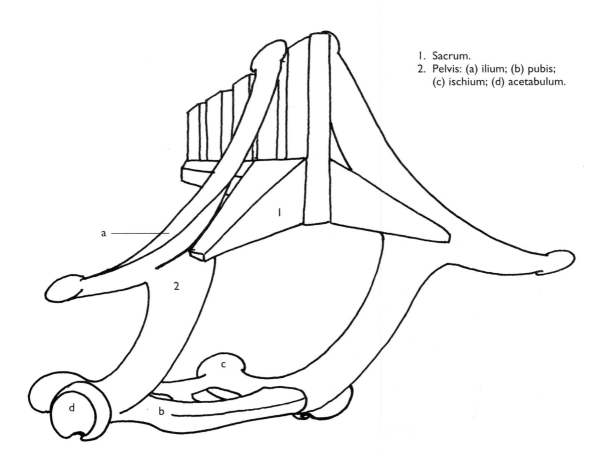

1. Sacrum.
2. Pelvis: (a) ilium; (b) pubis; (c) ischium; (d) acetabulum.

If this representation looks less like the familiar image of the horse's pelvic skeleton and more like a roof truss supported by a sled with castors, that is intentional.

When we look at the horse's hindquarters, most of us, quite rightly, are concerned with the condition of the muscles. After all, they are the source of impulsion and the foundation of self-carriage. However, beneath the muscular mass is a very important bony structure, which unfortunately is often disregarded until it causes problems.

The bones of the pelvic girdle have the most difficult task. To riders, their purpose is to support the overlying muscles, whereas arguably their more important function is to protect the internal organs. On the one hand, the bones have to form a solid housing, so that the soft inner organs are not crushed by the power of the muscles. On the other hand, their shape needs to be suitably dynamic to tolerate different levels of movement. Both physically and biologically speaking, the pelvis is the place where 'push comes to shove'.

In summary, the entire construction has to accommodate a waste disposal system, and in the case of the mare a birth channel, while at the same time it has to propel the body onwards and upwards, taking the power generated by muscles of the hind limb and passing it on to muscles either side of the horse's spine. In other words, it's a multi-purpose building with a rigid framework and flexible design.

13. The sacroiliac joint.

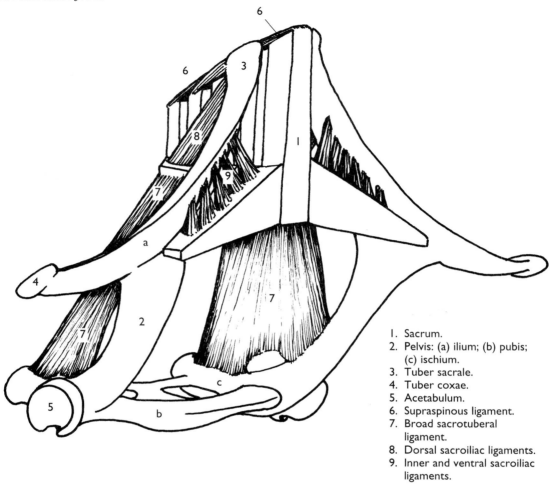

1. Sacrum.
2. Pelvis: (a) ilium; (b) pubis; (c) ischium.
3. Tuber sacrale.
4. Tuber coxae.
5. Acetabulum.
6. Supraspinous ligament.
7. Broad sacrotuberal ligament.
8. Dorsal sacroiliac ligaments.
9. Inner and ventral sacroiliac ligaments.

The pelvis consists of three bones – ilium, pubis, and ischium – which, in the adult animal are fused into one complete unit. Similarly, the sacrum, which is a continuation of the spine, consists of five vertebrae fused together. Somehow, pelvis and sacrum have to be joined.

The sacrum provides the roof of the pelvic building. The first element of the sacrum – the most substantial part – has two powerful, almost horizontal 'arms'. The left and right ilial portions of the pelvis, which are drawn out like the antlers of a moose, rest on the arms of the sacrum. The two parts are held in place by connective tissue and strong fibrous bands. This diagram is exploded to show the ligaments but, in reality, this gap is no more than a slit.

The moulded upper surface of the ilium is filled with the muscles that transfer the movement from the hindquarters towards the lumbar spine. The broad, sacrotuberal ligaments together form a tent that separates the deep muscles and sciatic nerve on the outside from the vital pelvic organs within.

In the horse's musculoskeletal system, there are many examples of sound engineering principles: the sacroiliac joint is perhaps not one of them. However, when it comes to riding with impulsion, the integrity of the sacroiliac joint is the bottom line.

*14. Ultimately, the sacroiliac ligaments are the only tissues
that attach the pelvis to the sacrum. Imagine what would
happen to the pelvic girdle without them.*

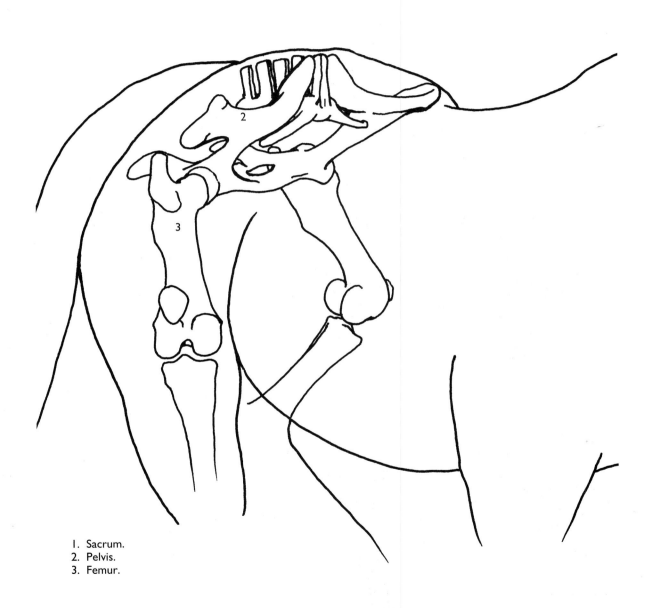

1. Sacrum.
2. Pelvis.
3. Femur.

15. The sacroiliac joint must remain intact, whatever the horse does: whether standing up on his hind legs ...

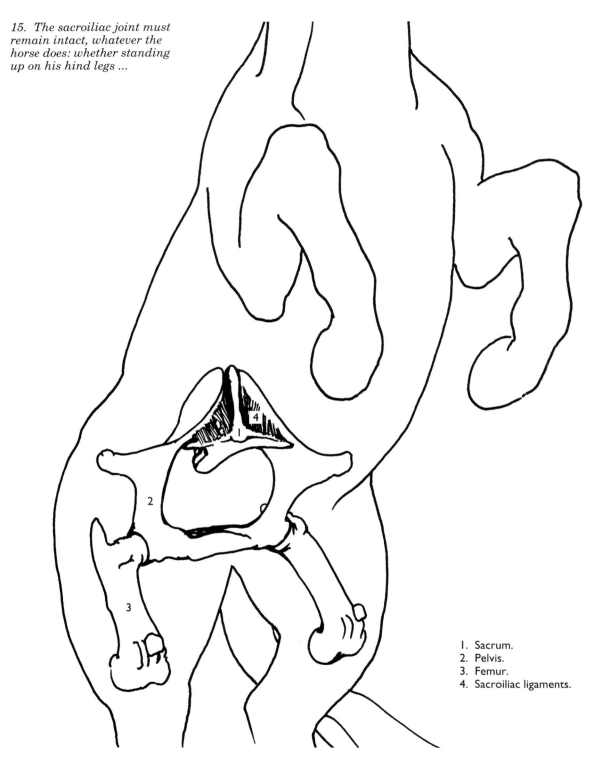

1. Sacrum.
2. Pelvis.
3. Femur.
4. Sacroiliac ligaments.

16. ... or lying down to have a good roll.

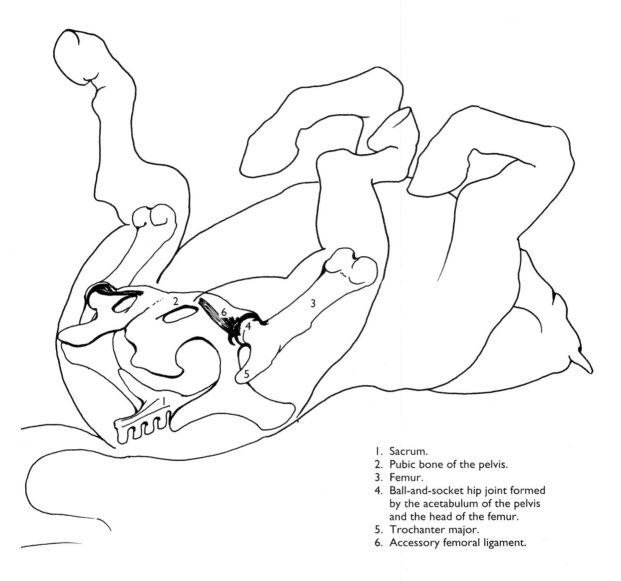

1. Sacrum.
2. Pubic bone of the pelvis.
3. Femur.
4. Ball-and-socket hip joint formed by the acetabulum of the pelvis and the head of the femur.
5. Trochanter major.
6. Accessory femoral ligament.

The spherical head of the femur articulates with the deep socket of the acetabulum, located at the junction of the three bones that form the pelvis. The accessory femoral ligament passes under a shorter transverse ligament to reach the 'ball' of this ball-and-socket joint. Although, by its shape, this joint should allow considerable rotation, in reality movement is limited by the strategic placing of the muscles.

17. *The anatomy of the stifle.*

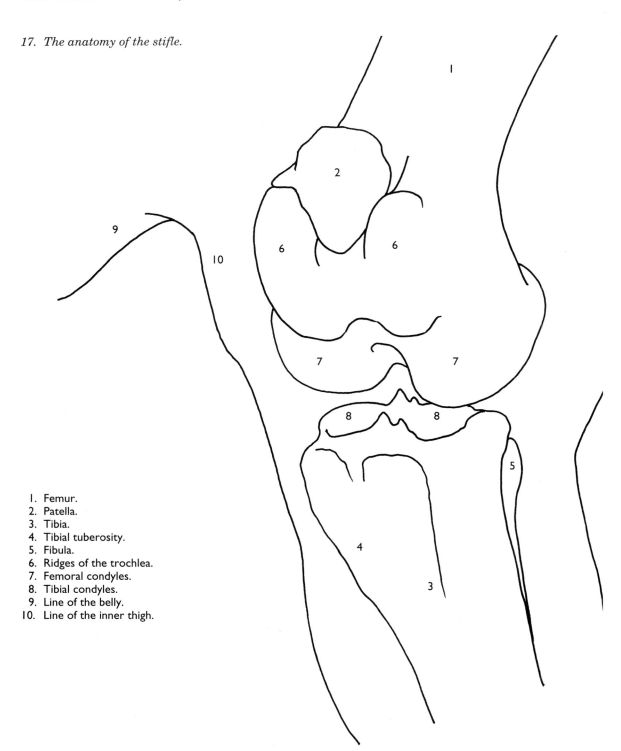

1. Femur.
2. Patella.
3. Tibia.
4. Tibial tuberosity.
5. Fibula.
6. Ridges of the trochlea.
7. Femoral condyles.
8. Tibial condyles.
9. Line of the belly.
10. Line of the inner thigh.

18. *The mechanical components of the stifle.*

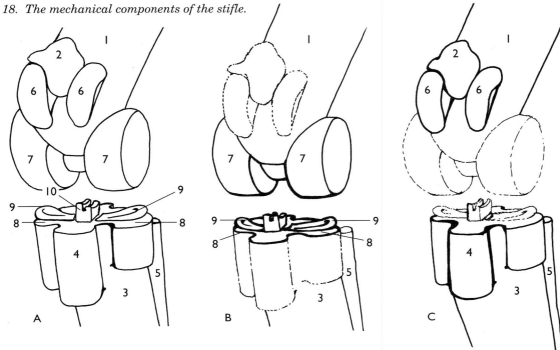

A. The complete stifle.
B. Components of the joint between the femur and tibia (strong black outlines).
C. Components of the joint between the femur and patella (strong black outlines).

1. Femur.
2. Patella.
3. Tibia.
4. Tibial tuberosity.
5. Fibula.
6. Ridges of the trochlea.
7. Femoral condyles.
8. Tibial condyles.
9. Menisci.
10. Intercondylar eminence.

The stifle joint causes problems not just to horses but also to horse people. It comprises a complicated arrangement of stays and pulleys that work absolutely smoothly when they are in balance, and jam the joint solid when they are not.

Muscles converge on the stifle joint from all directions, although few actually insert on the bones themselves. Nevertheless, the muscles conceal the fact that the stifle mechanism consists of not one joint but two. The first joint is between the femur and the tibia; the second is between the femur and the patella.

The end of the femur has two distinctive sets of features. Firstly, there is a pair of large, round processes called condyles which steamroller their way backwards and forwards across the joint surface of the tibia. Secondly, there is a pair of ridges, collectively called a trochlea. This is part of a pulley system, and provides a track for the patella. The condyles of the femur are round and the articulating surface of the tibia is, by comparison, almost flat and horizontal. It is clear that, unlike most joints, these shapes do not correspond. Therefore, to create a matching joint, mandarin-segment shaped cushions, called menisci, are inserted between the two bones.

The tibial joint surface is divided into two parts (unfortunately also called condyles), and there is a raised area of bone in the centre, called the intercondylar eminence. This separates the two menisci and provides an important place of attachment for ligaments.

The top of the tibia is strengthened by bony buttresses, not unlike those surrounding the humerus in the forelimb. The foremost of these is called the tibial tuberosity and can easily be felt just under the skin.

19. The stifle joint: a hinge and a half!

The horse's stifle bears the brunt of the huge forces generated by the powerful muscles of the hindquarters. As a joint it must concertina and pivot, allowing the horse to lift his forehand from the ground and turn his body to one side, sometimes all within a matter of seconds.

If this was the only purpose of the stifle, a straightforward hinge that allowed a small amount of lateral rotation (as, for example, the pastern does), would be sufficient. However, such a structure would simply collapse when the horse was standing still, or dozing, because of the angle of the limb. The horse would have to use extra muscle power to fix the joint, or else the joint would have to be restrained by providing it with a special locking device. In fact, the stifle mechanism is a hinge, but it is a self-locking hinge with a quick-release system.

The condyles of the femur roll on the horizontal surface of the tibia, cushioned by the menisci. The bones of the femur and tibia are held in strict alignment by collateral ligaments, one on each side of the joint (laterally and medially). The menisci are prevented from slipping away from the tibia by short ligaments which attach them to the area of the central bony eminence. The femoral condyles are prevented from sliding off the menisci by two crossed (cruciate) ligaments, which also attach close to the same area.

Most joints do not need internal fixation. However, because the femoral and tibial condyles do not correspond in shape, ligaments are required inside the stifle (femorotibial) joint to act as a safety net. Nevertheless, this should not disguise the fact that the joint operates as a hinge mechanism.

With the patella it is quite a different story. The patella is a small bone covered with cartilage. It rests in the groove of the trochlea and is located underneath the end of the quadriceps femoris muscle. In effect, the patella is a solid ball-bearing in a flexible case that glides between the trochleal ridges in response to the muscle's movement.

The end of the quadriceps femoris muscle feeds into the middle patellar ligament, which inserts in the groove of the tibial tuberosity. There are two additional patellar ligaments, one lateral and one medial, that also insert at the tibial tuberosity. They originate from the patellar cartilage. The patella is aligned with the trochleal groove by the help of ligaments from the femoral condyles.

When the horse is moving, and the quadriceps muscle is operational, the patella secures the passage of the muscle over the ridges of the trochlea. However, when the horse is resting, the patella becomes a labour-saving device. By raising one hip, the horse can cause the quadriceps muscle to lift the patella into a position above, and slightly to the inside of, the medial trochleal ridge. This locks the hinge and, in conjunction with the reciprocal apparatus to the hock (see Chapter 3, page 77), fixes the limb so that it becomes self-supporting. The other hind leg can rest on its toe and go to sleep.

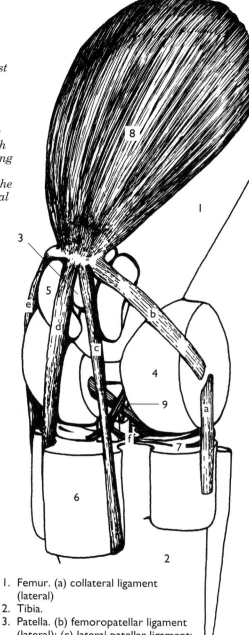

1. Femur. (a) collateral ligament (lateral)
2. Tibia.
3. Patella. (b) femoropatellar ligament (lateral); (c) lateral patellar ligament; (d) middle patellar ligament; (e) medial patellar ligament.
4. Lateral femoral condyle.
5. Trochlea (medial ridge).
6. Tibial tuberosity.
7. Meniscus. (f) ligaments of the menisci.
8. Quadriceps femoris muscle.
9. Cruciate ligaments.

30

A. Right hock.
B. Left hock.

1. Tibia.
2. Cannon (or third metatarsal) bone.
3. Calcaneus.
4. Talus.
5. Central tarsal bone.
6. Third tarsal bone.
7. Fourth tarsal bone.
8. First and second tarsal bones (fused).
9. Splint (or second metatarsal) bone.

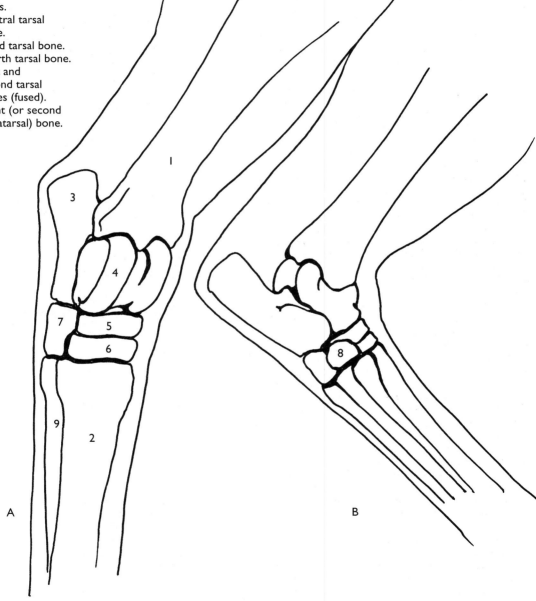

20. The anatomy of the hock.

31

21. Yes, it's another hinge.

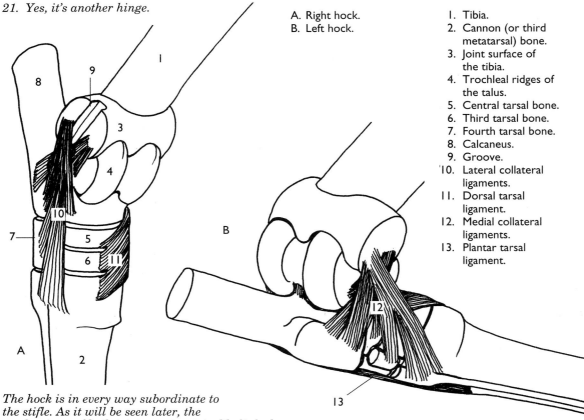

A. Right hock.
B. Left hock.

1. Tibia.
2. Cannon (or third metatarsal) bone.
3. Joint surface of the tibia.
4. Trochleal ridges of the talus.
5. Central tarsal bone.
6. Third tarsal bone.
7. Fourth tarsal bone.
8. Calcaneus.
9. Groove.
10. Lateral collateral ligaments.
11. Dorsal tarsal ligament.
12. Medial collateral ligaments.
13. Plantar tarsal ligament.

The hock is in every way subordinate to the stifle. As it will be seen later, the mechanisms of both joints are inextricably linked: one cannot move without the other. However, although the hock joint is a hinge, if it moved in a straight line the lower limb would knock into the horse's belly during flexion. For this reason, an important feature of the hock joint is the trochlea. This forms part of the bone known as the talus.

The trochlea of the talus articulates with the joint surface at the lower end of the tibia. This is moulded so that it exactly fits over the two trochleal ridges. As the joint flexes, the lower limb is automatically pulled to one side because the trochleal ridges slant outwards. In this way, the rear hoof avoids hitting the abdomen.

The base of the talus stands on a stack of small tarsal bones which ultimately rests on the cannon (or third metatarsal) bone. There should be no movement between any of these lower bones and, to ensure this, they are strapped together by collateral and dorsal ligaments. The fan-shaped configuration of the collateral ligaments is designed to help return the hinge to its original position during movement. (The attachment of the lateral collateral ligament on the side of the tibia is divided by a groove in the bone which provides a channel for the tendon of the lateral digital extensor muscle.)

When thinking of the hock, most horse people will visualize the shape of the point of the hock, which is created largely by the bone called the calcaneus. This has a lever-like extension, similar to the olecranon at the elbow, which is an important site for muscle and tendon insertion. It is the equivalent of the human heel.

Like the talus, the calcaneus is supported by the stack of tarsal bones which, to the rear, rests partially on the splint (or second and fourth tarsal) bones. A ligament – called the plantar tarsal ligament – extends down the rear surface of the hock, and it is weaknesses here that become undeniably visible as curbs.

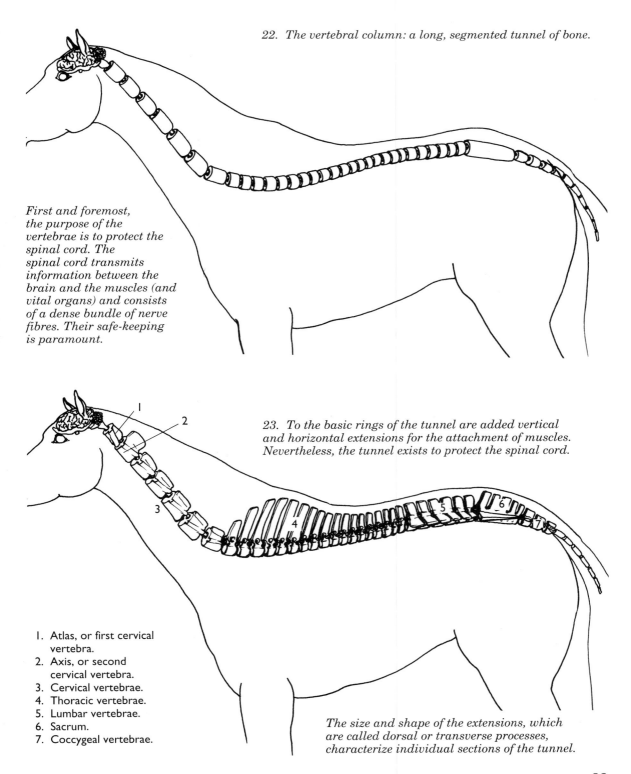

22. *The vertebral column: a long, segmented tunnel of bone.*

First and foremost, the purpose of the vertebrae is to protect the spinal cord. The spinal cord transmits information between the brain and the muscles (and vital organs) and consists of a dense bundle of nerve fibres. Their safe-keeping is paramount.

23. To the basic rings of the tunnel are added vertical and horizontal extensions for the attachment of muscles. Nevertheless, the tunnel exists to protect the spinal cord.

1. Atlas, or first cervical vertebra.
2. Axis, or second cervical vertebra.
3. Cervical vertebrae.
4. Thoracic vertebrae.
5. Lumbar vertebrae.
6. Sacrum.
7. Coccygeal vertebrae.

The size and shape of the extensions, which are called dorsal or transverse processes, characterize individual sections of the tunnel.

1. Nuchal ligament.
2. Laminae of the nuchal ligament.
3. Supraspinous ligament.
4. Interspinous ligaments.
5. Intertransverse ligaments.
6. Ventral longitudinal ligament.

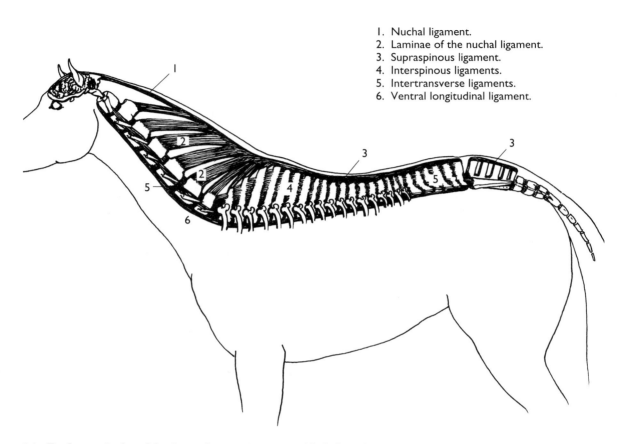

24. To the vertical and horizontal extensions are added short ligaments. Long ligaments span the length of the tunnel, above, below, and inside. The object is to stabilize the spine under the action of the muscles.

25. *Ligaments: unsung heroes of the horse's musculoskeletal system.*

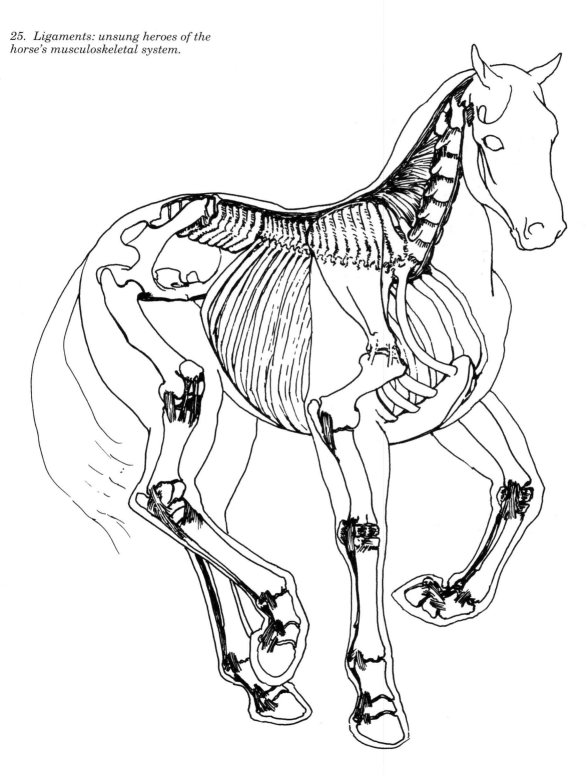

3 The Driving Forces: Muscles

At the sixth neck vertebra, the front aspect of each transverse process is irregular. There is also an increased uptake of radioisotope in the vertebral bodies of the rear thoracic spine. However, these findings are probably within the normal range since they occur in many normal riding horses.

This was the gist of a conversation summarizing the results of a bone-scan and series of X-rays that were carried out as part of a clinical investigation. The horse in question had serious, probably pain-related, behavioural problems (for example, panic bolting). Yet, despite the fact that these changes affected the bones of the spine, they were not placed at the top of the diagnostic leader board. Instead, first in the line-up was the sacroiliac joint because, here, the bone-scan readings were even higher.

Diagnostically, this horse's symptoms were attributed to one pathological cause, namely severe inflammation of the sacroiliac joint. The question is, how far did the roughened edges of the neck vertebra, or the remodelling of the bones in the mid-back (approximately under the cantle of the saddle) predispose the horse to this inflammation? Was it right to dismiss these findings as incidental? Or should they have been held accountable? Sadly, it was not possible to turn the clock back for this horse, and he was prescribed a long course of Bute. Nevertheless, in giving precedence to a single piece of clinical evidence, do we not run the risk of creating diagnostic scapegoats?

For example, we might decide to point the finger at the sacroiliac joint because, here, the symptoms of strain are more spectacular (rearing, bolting, napping) than they are in the mid-back or neck (stiffness or stumbling). But are we justified in drawing a line under this diagnosis, and making it the arbitrary cut-off point between normality and abnormality? Can we arrange the signs of permanent physical damage along a hypothetical yardstick and declare that some are normal whereas others are not?

In medical jargon, the word normal is a clinical definition. It is used to describe any state that has no diagnostic significance — normal temperature, normal heart rate, normal white-cell count, and so on. However, words have associated meanings, and the word normal has more than most. For example, igloos are normal dwellings if you are an Eskimo, tents are normal if you are a nomad, fasting is normal if you belong to a certain religion, and even earthquakes are normal if you happen to live in an earthquake zone. Therefore, normal is not definitive, it is a sliding scale. More importantly, it implies acceptability. In other words, degenerative changes to the spine may be normal in the clinical sense, but does this make them acceptable in the body of the ridden horse?

Clinical diagnosis is a form of judgement. It has to be in order to provide the basis for treatment. However, there is a difference between exercising judgement and being judgemental, and it is not the role of veterinary surgeons, or doctors, to be judgemental. On the contrary, theirs is a duty of care, fighting the known symptoms of disease. It is a straightforward contest: man versus the germs, man versus the vulnerability of the flesh. The weapons consist of medication and surgery, and they are forged through the process of learning how disease attacks the body. It would only throw the battle into confusion if vets and doctors also had to confront the question why. Therefore, when it comes to treating musculoskeletal problems in the horse, the focus is on resolving changes that have already taken place (for example, in the bones or joints), not on speculating about the chain of events that may have precipitated these changes.

However, this ethos influences the way we view lameness. We look at lameness as if it were a window on a single event rather than the door to an ongoing situation. In reality, many lamenesses are launched only after there has been a long countdown of unsoundness.

The distinction between lameness and soundness should be as clear as black and white. On the one hand we have a sound horse, on the other we have a lame horse: nothing could be simpler than that. It should not be necessary to nominate a grey area for horses that are neither lame nor sound. Unfortunately, this assumes that we can define soundness as a single aspect of mobility, which of course we can't.

Soundness depends on the physical build, aptitude and, to some extent, mental flexibility of the individual. It is a qualitative description, and may even reflect age or immaturity. For example, young horses pass through phases of awkward movement, bordering on unsoundness, as their limbs and bodies grow or as they learn to adjust their balance when they are first backed. When they move up the competition ladder, their training becomes more specific, and their muscles become more finely tuned to the specialized needs of one sport. Horses, like all athletes, acquire different physical proportions. But whereas every athlete has to achieve a certain level of fitness to be successful, when it comes to soundness there is simply no universal starting-block.

It is fair to say that no horse enjoys being lame. In fact, most horses apparently go to tremendous lengths to preserve the appearance of soundness. Whether or not this behaviour is rooted in the basic instinct for survival, it seems that many horses try to get about as naturally as possible, both when they are suffering from injury and even when they have acutely painful conditions such as infections in the foot, until, of course, the pressure makes this impossible.

When the musculoskeletal system is threatened by injury or disease, there is only one way the horse can help himself and that is by adjusting the balance of the muscles. In the case of acute trauma – a hard knock or wrench, perhaps – local muscles tense up and take the injured part of the body out of commission. It is a temporary solution, and one that is usually reversible.

However, there is a more insidious type of trauma, for example an ache or soreness. To relieve the pain of an aching joint or sore ligament, the muscles tighten. The effect is not as obvious or pronounced as it is in the case of a serious injury. Nevertheless, the body still takes steps to protect itself because an ache is the precursor of strain and therefore represents an area of weakness.

Aches and soreness are types of dull pain: they are not usually associated with gross tissue damage. However, even dull pain needs time to resolve, and, unless it disappears completely, its presence constantly causes the muscles to compensate. Inevitably, compensation becomes a habit, and the result is one of permanently incorrect movement.

In humans, experience tells us that when muscles are habitually used incorrectly (for example, lop-sidedly) the muscles themselves become painful. We can assume that it is equally so in horses. Consequently, if the horse has to continually brace himself in order to relieve sore joints, the pain must one day spread to the muscles. When there is no further protective mechanism available, the horse goes lame.

Whenever lameness is preceded by a long period of muscular tension, the pain becomes chronic. Chronic pain may be less penetrating than acute pain, but it is more insistent: a constant, nagging reminder, rather than a short, sharp telling-off. It permeates the tissues, often making it difficult to locate the exact source. Yet horses, like humans, learn to live with it.

Chronic musculoskeletal pain is always indicative of change: change in the use of the system, change in the nature of its construction. Whether it is owed to ageing, or to continual misuse, the musculoskeletal system undergoes change (principally, degeneration) in both the substance and structure of its tissues. However, these changes take different lengths of time to materialize. In fact, they are rather like the transformations in a geological landscape.

Imagine that the musculoskeletal tissues are divided into three layers. The most superficial layer contains the muscles and tendons. Their contours, like the sands of a desert, are quickly built up, and just as quickly eroded, by the external forces of nature. Below this, in the middle layer, are the ligaments. They are automatically affected by the shifting status of the muscles, but the transformations are slower, and, like any underground system, their structural importance becomes apparent only when they begin to give way.

Finally, beneath both of these is the bedrock of the bones. Every pressure exerted by the body comes to bear here. However, like the deformation of the hardest rocks, it takes time and considerable effort to change the face of bones. But change they do, and the culmination can be read as clearly as the strata of an exposed cliff face: an unmistakable and permanent record of the way the bones have been used in movement.

Therefore, in the context of the horse's body, findings such as roughened transverse processes and remodelled vertebrae do not constitute major geological upheavals in the way that severe inflammation of the sacroiliac joint does. They are more the result of 'constant dripping that wears away the stone'. Nevertheless, bones do not wear themselves away. This erosion is caused by muscles. And what makes muscles act on the bones in this way? In the case of the sixth neck vertebra, and vertebrae in the mid-back, the answer probably lies in riding the horse on the forehand.

In his natural state, the horse spends a great deal of time on the forehand, both when he is grazing and when he is moving at speed. His muscles and bones are perfectly capable of surviving a natural equine existence. The forehand becomes an issue only when the horse is ridden. The horse's body is not designed to carry the additional weight of a rider over the forelegs because most of his own weight is already carried here. The only way we can ride the horse without causing him permanent damage is by utilizing the way in which he, himself, raises the forehand off the ground: namely by using the muscles of the back and of the hind limbs.

The muscle system either side of the horse's spine begins at the sacrum, attaches to the spine in a gradual arc, and sweeps down under the shoulder blades to insert at the base of the neck. From this area, between the first ribs and the last neck vertebra, the same muscle system describes a second arc that rises up to the horse's poll.

To describe the action of these muscles, we should imagine a ride on a 'big dipper'. The energy of their movement is represented by the car. It sets out from the hindquarters with sufficient impulsion to drive it up and over the back, and down the gradient to the base of the neck. From here, the momentum sustains the passage of the car until it reaches the highest point of the neck, and allows it to return via the chest and abdominal muscles to the quarters, where the circuit begins anew.

The successful operation of the horse's back muscles and, for that matter, the 'big dipper', depends on exact timing and precise engineering. Not many people would want to ride a switch-back if the cars always got stuck at the highest point or came to a grinding halt at the bottom of the best slope. One might even suggest that if this happened regularly, the rails would begin to wear out at strategic points, not unlike certain places along the horse's spine.

Unfortunately, nobody can ask for their money back if the energy gets stuck over the horse's back or at the base of the neck, least of all the horse. And if the muscles do not fire in the correct sequence, the vertebrae are likely to show signs of wear. Degenerative changes in the bones of the horse's back? That would be a sad indictment of the way we ride. Of course, it does not have to be this way if we ride the horse allowing his muscles to work as they were intended.

THE TERMINOLOGY OF MUSCLE MOVEMENT

In daily, practical activities with the horse, it is sufficient to describe the limbs as moving forwards or backwards, up or down, inwards and outwards, especially if we are standing next to the horse in an arena. It is usually obvious from the situation which part of the limb is being referred to. Nevertheless, these terms are not accurate descriptions of the way individual muscles move: they are either too broad or they rely on every onlooker sharing the same vantage point.

The movement of a muscle is strictly limited by its size, shape, and placement in relation to the skeleton, in the same way that the movement of a joint is limited by the joint's shape. In the first instance, all muscles share the same basic principles of construction. The muscle fibres are individually wrapped in fine nets of connective tissue and then bound together into small groups by sleeves of connective tissue. These are bound again into larger bundles, and the whole is completely encased by a covering of connective tissue to form a single muscle.

The protective layers of connective tissue, which comprise a stocking-like mesh, enable the muscle fibres to glide past each other, as different parts of the muscle contract. Each layer contains elastic fibres, and these, together with the contractile fibres of the muscle tissue, feed into the fibres of the tendons. A tendon is placed at each end of the muscle, and it is via the tendons that all muscles are connected to the bones.

One muscle connects at least two separate bones, and spans one or more joints. The places of attachment are technically called 'origin' and 'insertion'. For the purpose of classifying the mode of action, we have to imagine that muscles have a beginning (origin) and an end (insertion), even though some shapes of muscles are surprisingly symmetrical, and certain muscles work in two directions depending on which part of the body is fixed (for example, head or shoulder, hindquarters or back). Nevertheless, muscles are regarded as moving one bone relative to the position of the other, rather than pulling both together.

In reality, the skeleton moves as a fluent whole rather than in individual sections. It is unlikely that any bone is completely stationary while an adjacent bone is being moved. However, in order to unravel the spaghetti-like threads of muscle movement, we have to apply the narrowest form of interpretation.

For this reason, the science of anatomy has chosen certain words to represent muscle movement. Unfortunately, some of the these words are misleading because they are used in everyday equestrian language (for example, extension). But we have to remember that, in the context of anatomy, the terminology is specific.

Although the bones contribute to movement by virtue of their passive weight, the anatomical terminology describes the active effect of muscles on the skeleton. In other words, it assumes that movement in any direction is the product of muscular intervention. (For example, it is true that, given time, the cannon bone would swing the fetlock forwards after the horse has bent the knee joint, but, if this were the only mechanism, it would be a fairly tedious means of progress.)

In movement, all bones create an angle at the joints, even where the bones are apparently positioned in a straight line. The apex of this angle may point in the direction of movement, or in the reverse direction. The muscles fill either the included space of the angle or they pass over the apex.

To produce movement, the muscles make the angle between two bones either narrower or wider. They then return the bones to their starting positions. If the shape of the joint allows, muscles may also move the bones sideways, either towards the body or away from it. However, rotation, which is a feature of movement in the human arm and leg, is barely possible in the horse's limbs, although some rotation does take place in small joints, such as those at the top of the ribs.

In the horse, there are four named directions of movement. Numbers 1 and 2 refer to the movement of the bones at a single joint. Numbers 3 and 4 refer to the movement of a limb in relation to the mid-line of the body:

1. Flexion (bending).
The angle at the joint is made narrower. Muscles that have the prime function of closing the angle of a joint are called flexors.

2. Extension (stretching).
The angle of the joint is widened. Muscles pass over the apex of the joint. These muscles are called extensors.

3. Adduction (drawing in).
Muscles draw the limb towards the mid-line of the body. These are called adductors.

4. Abduction (leading away).
Muscles lead the limb away from the mid-line of the body. These are called abductors.

There is one named abductor muscle in the horse – abductor pollicis longus – called after its counterpart in humans. However, in the horse, this muscle has no abductor function. On the other hand, there are muscles around the top of the horse's limbs that fulfil the function of abductors, even though they are not so called.

In riding, we commonly talk about extension when we mean lengthened stride. Similarly, the flexion tests that are used to identify lameness may specifically bend some joints but at the same time actually stretch others. We should remember that, in the anatomical sense, flexion and extension apply only to individual joints. If we want to describe the forwards and backwards motion of the whole limb, it is more appropriate to refer to it as protraction and retraction.

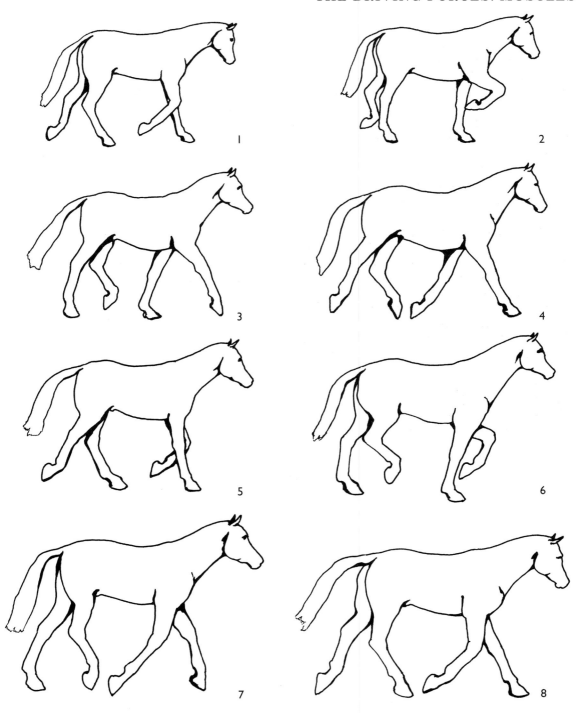

26. *One stride of the trot: a sequence of movements. In this example, we can follow the right forelimb through a sequence of movements from picture 1 through to picture 8. The culmination of this sequence is that the horse's body is moved forward by one stride. To complete the stride, the leg must pass through different phases of flexion and extension.*

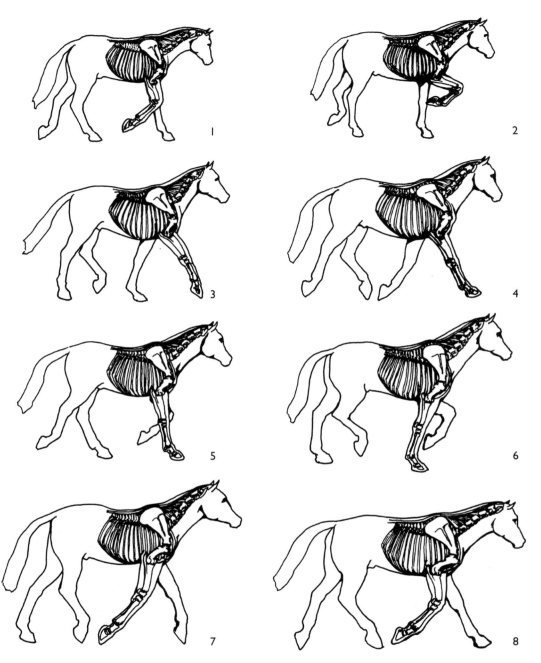

27. One stride of the trot: the changing angles of the bones and joints.
     The bones of the right forelimb are shown against the bones of the ribcage and neck.
From picture 1 to picture 8 we can follow the phases of flexion and extension as they affect
the forelimb skeleton. In picture 2 the angle of the shoulder joint is wide (extension) while the
angles of all the subsequent joints are at their narrowest (maximum flexion). In picture 3 the
angle of the elbow joint is still narrow (flexion), whereas the angles of the joints in the lower
limb have almost completely opened (approaching extension). From pictures 7 to 8, the angle
of the shoulder joint becomes narrower (flexion), the angle of the elbow joint makes the
transition from wide to narrow (passing from extension to flexion) and the angles of the lower
joints begin to narrow again (approaching flexion).

42

28. *One stride of the trot: the changing emphasis of the muscles.*

Many of the muscles of the forelimb are clearly visible when the horse is trotting. However, in the same sequence of movements (pictures 1 to 8) we can see that, in order to move the body forwards, the horse has to use not only the muscles of the limb but also those of the neck and lower chest. The forelimb is not attached by a joint to the body wall. It relies on the action of the chest and neck muscles to swing the limb forwards and support the body as the foot hits the ground. In horses that are ridden on the forehand, the muscles at the base of the neck and lowest part of the chest are continually braced. Eventually these muscles become painful and the horse becomes unsound.

29. The supraspinatus muscle.

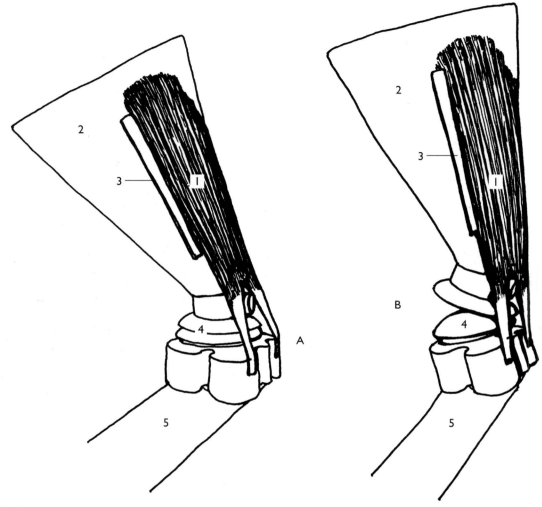

1. Supraspinatus muscle.
2. Scapula.
3. Scapula spine.
4. Shoulder joint.
5. Humerus.

This muscle begins close to the top of the scapula, or shoulder blade, and fills the space to the front of the scapula spine. It reaches over the apex of the joint angle, just above the narrow neck of the scapula, and attaches by means of two tendons to the buttress-like protrusions (greater and lesser tubercles) of the humerus.

The tendons of this muscle double up as ligaments to stabilize the front aspect of the shoulder joint (A). The action of the muscle extends the shoulder joint (widens the angle) (B).

N.B. In the geometric representation of bones and joints – here and in the following drawings – only those features that are relevant to the illustration are included.

30. *The deltoid muscle.*

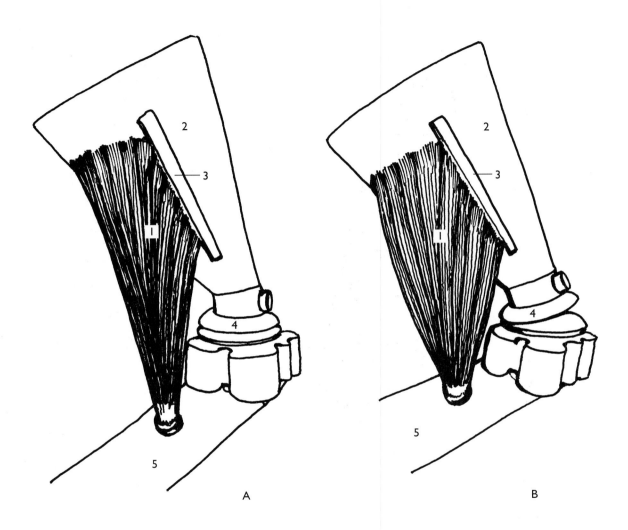

A   B

1. Deltoid muscle.
2. Scapula.
3. Scapula spine.
4. Shoulder joint.
5. Humerus.

This muscle takes its name from the delta shape and threefold attachments of the same muscle in humans. In horses, the muscle attaches along the lower side of the scapula spine and the adjacent surface of the scapula bone. It inserts at the humerus on a specially formed protuberance of bone called the deltoid tuberosity.

The action of this muscle flexes the shoulder joint (narrows the angle from the position in picture A to the position in picture B). The deltoid muscle can often be felt as a pronounced vertical ridge of muscle just to the rear of the shoulder joint.

31. The infraspinatus muscle.

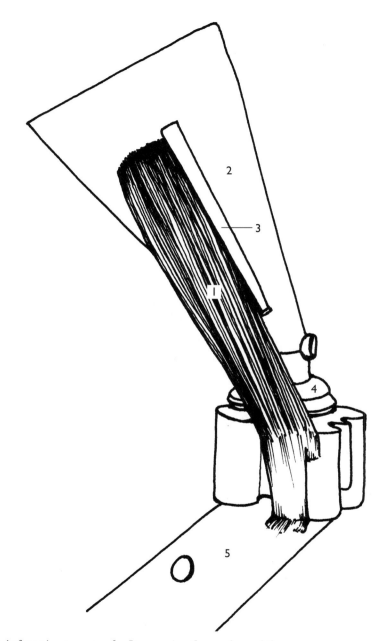

1. Infraspinatus muscle.
2. Scapula.
3. Scapula spine.
4. Shoulder joint.
5. Humerus.

Beneath the deltoid muscle lies the infraspinatus muscle. It occupies the surface of the scapula, on the lower side of the scapula spine, and inserts on the outer (lateral) side of the humerus.

Although the infraspinatus muscle works with the deltoid muscle in flexing the shoulder, its most important role – in the absence of collateral ligaments – is to hold the joint in alignment.

32. *The biceps brachii muscle.*

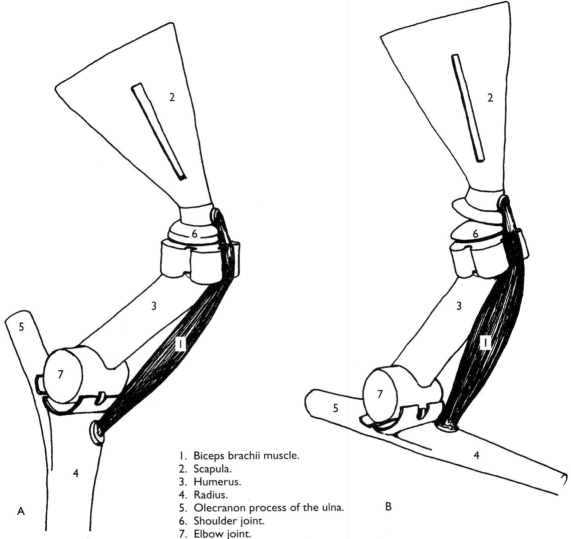

1. Biceps brachii muscle.
2. Scapula.
3. Humerus.
4. Radius.
5. Olecranon process of the ulna.
6. Shoulder joint.
7. Elbow joint.

A   B

The biceps muscle is so called because, in humans, the same muscle has two places of origin (two heads). In animals, however, the biceps muscle has only one origin. The word brachii (arm) is added to distinguish this muscle from one bearing the same name in the hind limb.

The biceps brachii acts on two joints, and, as it will be seen later, has a lateral extension that helps to control a third. The origin of the muscle is at the special protuberance of the scapula called the supraglenoid tubercle. The top tendon of the biceps lies in a groove between the 'buttresses' of the humerus, and the muscle inserts via a tendon at a protuberance on the front of the radius called the radial tuberosity.

As with the supraspinatus muscle, the tendon of the biceps brachii helps to stabilize the shoulder joint (A). The muscle extends the shoulder joint, but flexes the elbow (B). (The muscle is protected from friction, as it passes over the apex of the shoulder joint, by a bursa. This is an enclosed sac of viscous fluid that cushions a muscle against a bone or joint.)

33. The brachialis muscle.

The action on the elbow joint by the biceps brachii muscle is aided by that of the brachialis muscle. The spiral conformation of the brachialis (arm) muscle increases lift while the biceps provides the strength.

The origin of the brachialis muscle is on the medial side of the humerus. The muscle winds to the lateral side of the humerus along a groove and inserts on the medial side of the radius.

The brachialis muscle flexes the elbow joint.

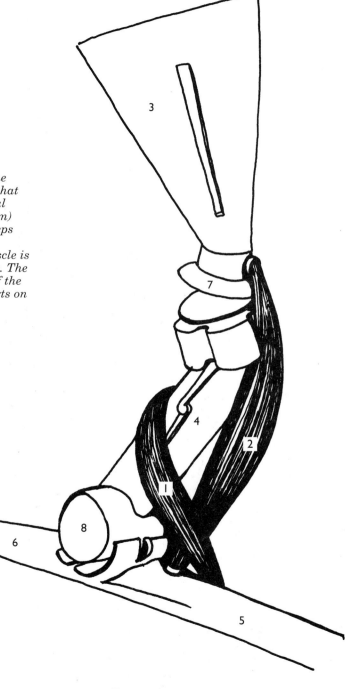

1. Brachialis muscle.
2. Biceps brachii muscle.
3. Scapula.
4. Humerus.
5. Radius.
6. Olecranon process of the ulna.
7. Shoulder joint.
8. Elbow joint.

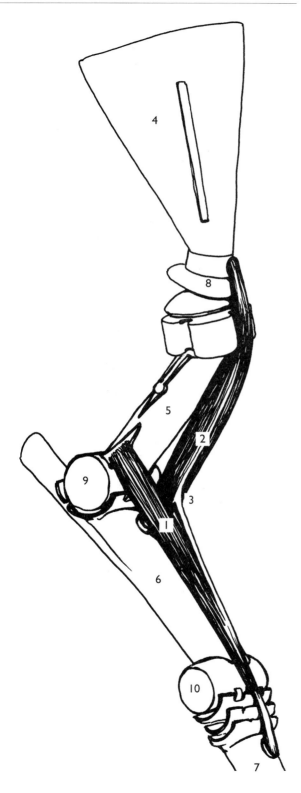

The origin of the extensor carpi radialis muscle is just above the elbow joint on a lateral ridge of bone called the lateral epicondyle. The insertion is just below the carpal joint (knee).

The biceps brachii muscle has a lateral tendon (called the lacertus fibrosus), which attaches to this muscle superficially and thereby links the action of the biceps to the carpus and lower leg. (The medial tendon of the biceps attaches to the radial tuberosity.)

The extensor carpi radialis muscle extends (opens the angle of) the carpal joint. Owing to the presence of the biceps and brachialis muscles and the lacertus fibrosus tendon, its action on the elbow joint is minimal. However, the extensor carpi radialis muscle plays an important role in stabilizing the carpal joint during the phase when the foot is touching the ground and the bodyweight is being propelled forwards. In horses that work on the forehand, this muscle becomes severely overdeveloped.

1. Extensor carpi radialis muscle.
2. Biceps brachii muscle.
3. Lacertus fibrosus (long tendon of the biceps brachii muscle).
4. Scapula.
5. Humerus.
6. Radius.
7. Third metacarpal (or cannon) bone.
8. Shoulder joint.
9. Elbow joint.
10. Carpal joint.

34. The extensor carpi radialis muscle.

35. *The triceps (brachii) muscle.*

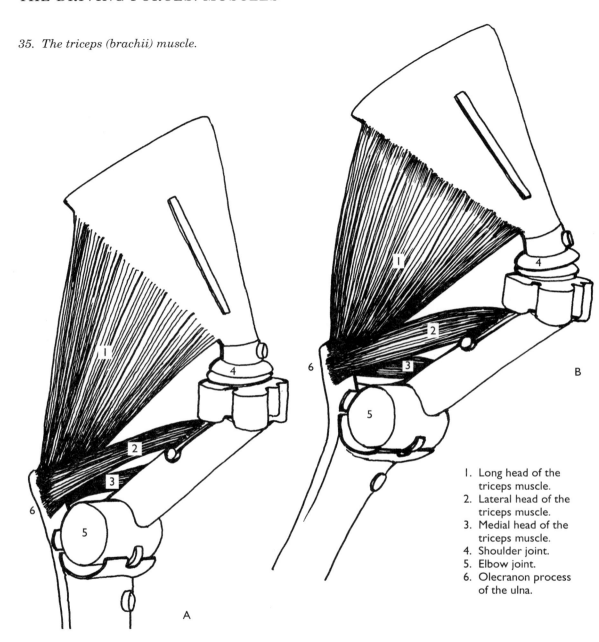

1. Long head of the triceps muscle.
2. Lateral head of the triceps muscle.
3. Medial head of the triceps muscle.
4. Shoulder joint.
5. Elbow joint.
6. Olecranon process of the ulna.

The triceps or three-headed muscle has three places of origin, namely along the rear border of the scapula (long head), on a ridge of bone along the lateral edge of the humerus (lateral head), and on the medial side of the humerus (medial head). The three parts of this muscle converge on the olecranon process of the ulna (6).

Working in combination, the three parts of the muscle extend the elbow joint (B). However, in the swing phase of a stride, the long head of the triceps helps to flex the shoulder joint. Because of the three-fold origins, this muscle also plays an important part in stabilizing the forelimb. Like the extensor carpi radialis, it is prone to overdevelopment in horses working on the forehand. It is often possible to feel hardened 'knots' of muscle tissue just above the olecranon process.

36. The lateral ulna, or extensor carpi ulnaris muscle.

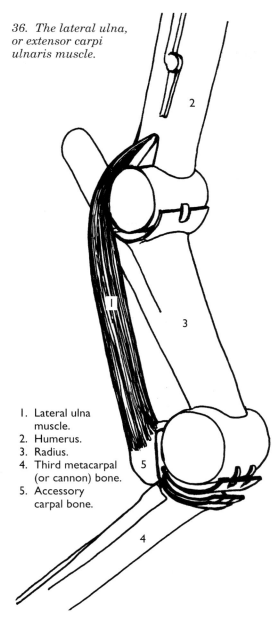

1. Lateral ulna muscle.
2. Humerus.
3. Radius.
4. Third metacarpal (or cannon) bone.
5. Accessory carpal bone.

37. Flexors of the carpal joint.

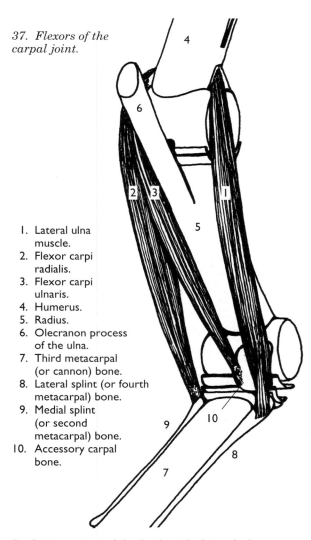

1. Lateral ulna muscle.
2. Flexor carpi radialis.
3. Flexor carpi ulnaris.
4. Humerus.
5. Radius.
6. Olecranon process of the ulna.
7. Third metacarpal (or cannon) bone.
8. Lateral splint (or fourth metacarpal) bone.
9. Medial splint (or second metacarpal) bone.
10. Accessory carpal bone.

In line with human anatomy, this muscle has been called the extensor carpi ulnaris because it fits into a neat scheme of two extensors and two flexors of the carpal joint. However, in the horse, this muscle is not an extensor, nor does it come from the ulna bone. The origin of the lateral ulna muscle is the lateral epicondyle of the humerus. It has two insertions. The first is on the accessory carpal bone.

This muscle flexes the carpal joint.

In this rear view of the foreleg, the lateral ulna muscle is shown again, this time with its second insertion on the head of the lateral splint bone. The flexor carpi radialis connects the medial epicondyle of the humerus to the medial splint bone. The flexor carpi ulnaris has two origins – on the olecranon process and on the medial epicondyle of the humerus – and it inserts on the accessory carpal bone. These three muscles flex the carpal joint.

The significance, and also the vulnerable situation, of the accessory bone can be seen. The many tendons and ligaments, which are in close proximity to the bone, are protected by lubricated sheaths. However, because the accessory carpal bone lies towards the outer (lateral) edge of the joint, any lateral/medial imbalance in the limb, including that caused by shoeing, can contribute to great soreness here.

38. The long flexor muscles and their tendons.

The superficial digital flexor muscle begins at the medial epicondyle of the humerus. This muscle is the origin of the superficial digital flexor tendon which is always distinctly visible under the skin of the horse's leg. The tendon passes between the two proximal sesamoid bones at the fetlock joint and divides to allow for the passage of the deep flexor tendon. The two branches insert mainly at the short pastern bone.

The deep digital flexor muscle has three origins: one on the medial epicondyle of the humerus, one on the medial surface of the olecranon, and one on the rear edge of the radius. This muscle is the origin of the deep digital flexor tendon. The deep flexor tendon passes between the two branches of the superficial flexor tendon, over the navicular bone, and inserts on the undersurface of the pedal or coffin bone.

Together, these muscles flex the joints of the foot and stabilize the fetlock joint.

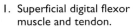

1. Superficial digital flexor muscle and tendon.
2. Deep digital flexor muscle and tendon.
3. Short pastern bone or middle phalanx.
4. Pedal (or coffin) bone, or distal phalanx.

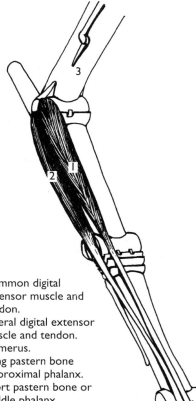

1. Common digital extensor muscle and tendon.
2. Lateral digital extensor muscle and tendon.
3. Humerus.
4. Long pastern bone or proximal phalanx.
5. Short pastern bone or middle phalanx.
6. Pedal (or coffin) bone, or distal phalanx.

39. The long extensor muscles and their tendons.

The common digital extensor muscle begins at the elbow joint, at the lower end of the humerus, as well as at the top of the radius. It is the origin of the extensor tendon, which inserts principally at the pedal bone.

The lateral digital extensor muscle begins at the side of the radius and partially at the ulna. It is the origin of the lateral extensor tendon, which crosses to the front aspect of the cannon bone and inserts at the long pastern bone.

These muscles extend the joints of the foot and stabilize the carpal joint.

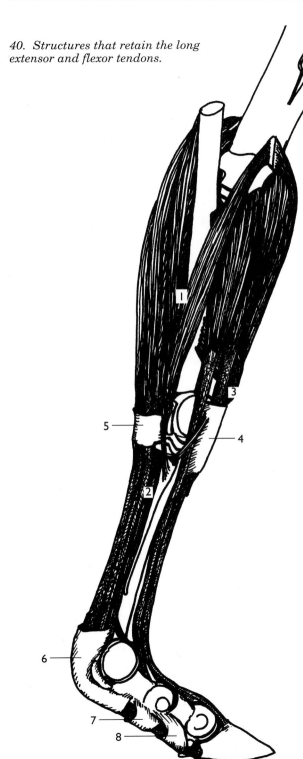

40. Structures that retain the long extensor and flexor tendons.

1. Site of the accessory radial (or 'superior') check ligament.
2. Site of the accessory carpal (or 'inferior') check ligament.
3. Abductor pollicis longus (extensor carpi obliquus) muscle.
4. Extensor retinaculum.
5. Flexor retinaculum.
6. Palmar anular ligament.
7. Proximal digital anular ligament.
8. Distal digital anular ligament.

From the preceding pictures it is clear that without retaining structures the tendons of the extensor and flexor muscles would simply flop about in space.

There are a number of ways in which the long muscles and tendons are retained. For example, the superficial digital flexor muscle takes up an accessory ('superior') check ligament from the radius. The deep digital flexor tendon, on the other hand, takes its accessory (or 'inferior') check ligament from the cannon bone. As it passes over the carpal joint, the common digital extensor tendon is held in place by a strap of connective tissue, called a retinaculum. A similar strap is provided for the flexor tendons at the back of the carpal joint.

There are three similar devices, on the underside of the fetlock and pastern, which are called anular ligaments.

These 'straps' along with the numerous ligaments ensure that the long tendons remain close to the bones and joints. The presence of these fixtures means that the tendons contribute to the stabilization of the limb, not just to its movement.

A small muscle passes diagonally across the extensor carpi radialis muscle. In humans, this would operate the thumb. Since the horse has no thumb, it simply adds stability to the extensor muscle and carpal joint.

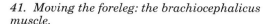

41. Moving the foreleg: the brachiocephalicus muscle.

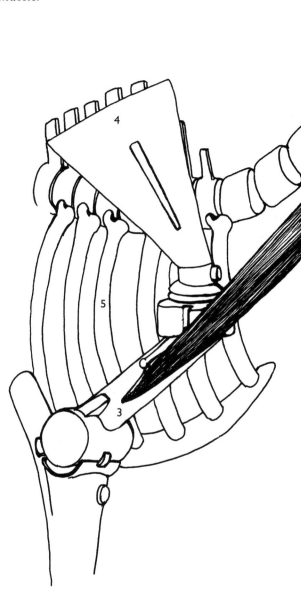

1. Brachiocephalicus muscle.
2. Mastoid process of the temporal bone (part of the skull).
3. Humerus.
4. Scapula.
5. Ribs.

The brachiocephalicus muscle (whose name means literally from arm to head) connects the skull of the horse with the upper part of the foreleg. The muscle begins close to the hinge of the jaw and attaches broadly to the humerus below the deltoid tuberosity. It therefore lies across the outside of the shoulder joint, with the biceps muscle to its inside and the brachialis muscle spiralling down immediately below.

This is one of the most important muscles in the horse's body, not because of what it does for the horse, but because of what it fails to do for the rider!

The brachiocephalicus muscle works in two ways. When the head and neck are fixed (by other muscles), it pulls the foreleg forwards. When the leg is fixed (for example in the stance phase of a stride) it pulls the neck downwards and the head back. (N.B. The word 'fix' is used deliberately. It should bring to the reader's mind the cardinal sin of riding the horse with a 'fixed' hand.)

In the freely moving horse, this muscle extends the reach of the foreleg. In the badly ridden horse, this muscle bears the brunt of the weight of the forehand. It becomes tense and unelastic, and eventually stops the horse from going anywhere at all.

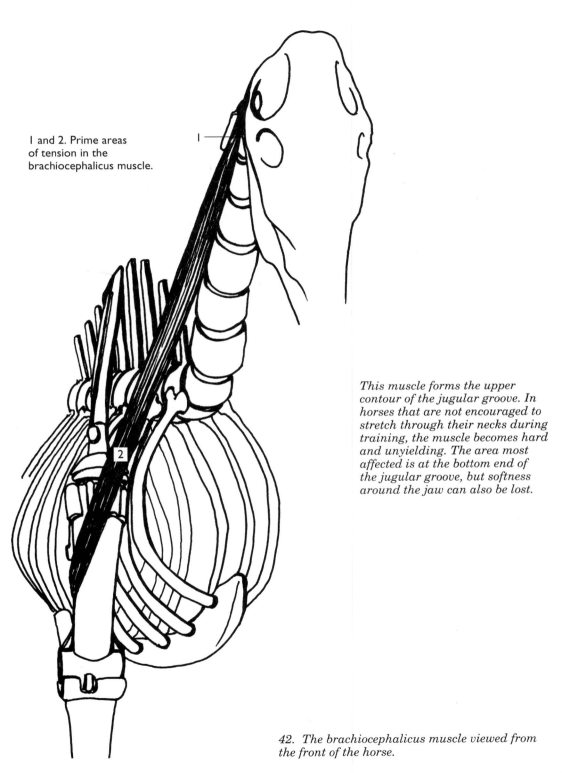

I and 2. Prime areas
of tension in the
brachiocephalicus muscle.

*This muscle forms the upper
contour of the jugular groove. In
horses that are not encouraged to
stretch through their necks during
training, the muscle becomes hard
and unyielding. The area most
affected is at the bottom end of
the jugular groove, but softness
around the jaw can also be lost.*

42. *The brachiocephalicus muscle viewed from
the front of the horse.*

43. *The omotransversarius muscle.*

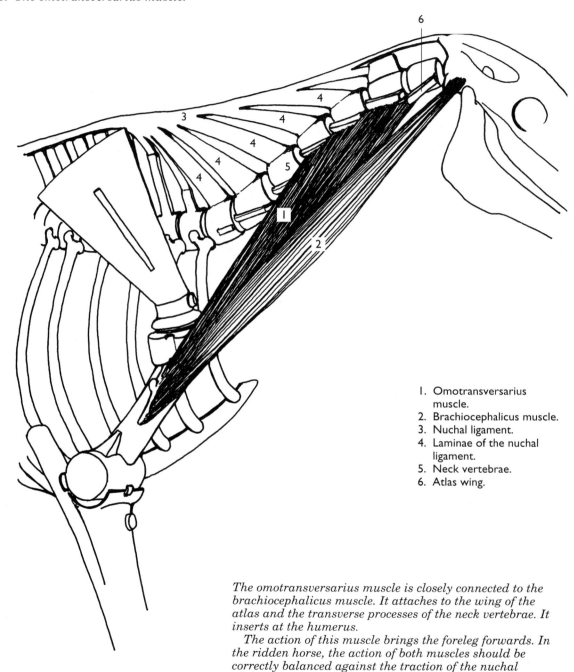

1. Omotransversarius muscle.
2. Brachiocephalicus muscle.
3. Nuchal ligament.
4. Laminae of the nuchal ligament.
5. Neck vertebrae.
6. Atlas wing.

The omotransversarius muscle is closely connected to the brachiocephalicus muscle. It attaches to the wing of the atlas and the transverse processes of the neck vertebrae. It inserts at the humerus.

The action of this muscle brings the foreleg forwards. In the ridden horse, the action of both muscles should be correctly balanced against the traction of the nuchal ligament and its laminae which attach to the neck bones.

44. The latissimus dorsi and teres major muscles.

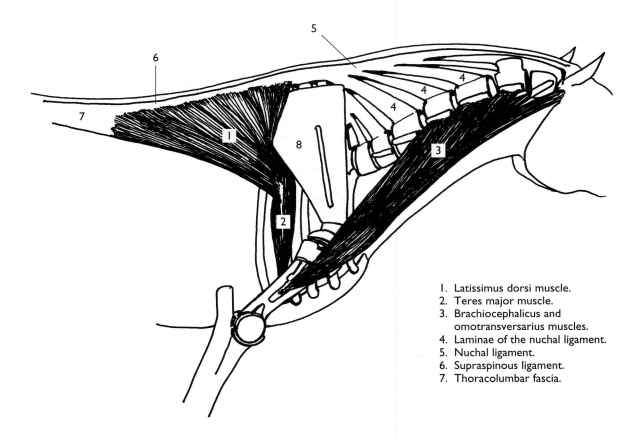

1. Latissimus dorsi muscle.
2. Teres major muscle.
3. Brachiocephalicus and omotransversarius muscles.
4. Laminae of the nuchal ligament.
5. Nuchal ligament.
6. Supraspinous ligament.
7. Thoracolumbar fascia.

The foreleg not only strides forward, it has to be drawn back so that the body can be propelled forwards. On the inside of the shoulder, between the forelimb and the ribcage, lies a muscle called the teres major. Its origin is on the underside of the scapula and it inserts on the medial side of the humerus.

This muscle flexes the shoulder joint.

The latissimus dorsi has a broad origin along the supraspinous ligament (which is the continuation of the nuchal ligament), and in a large expanse of connective tissue called the thoracolumbar fascia. It wraps over the rear edge of the scapula and uses the tendon of the teres major muscle to link it to the humerus.

The latissimus dorsi and teres major muscles between them draw the limb backwards, flexing the shoulder joint at the same time. The fan-like spread of the latissimus dorsi muscle also prevents the horse's body from buckling upwards when it is pulling forwards or pulling a heavy load.

If the nuchal ligament and its laminae are the counterbalance to the brachiocephalicus and omotransversarius muscles, the latissimus dorsi muscle is the counterpoise to both of these. Not, however, if the corner of the scapula is wedged under the tree of a tightly fitting saddle.

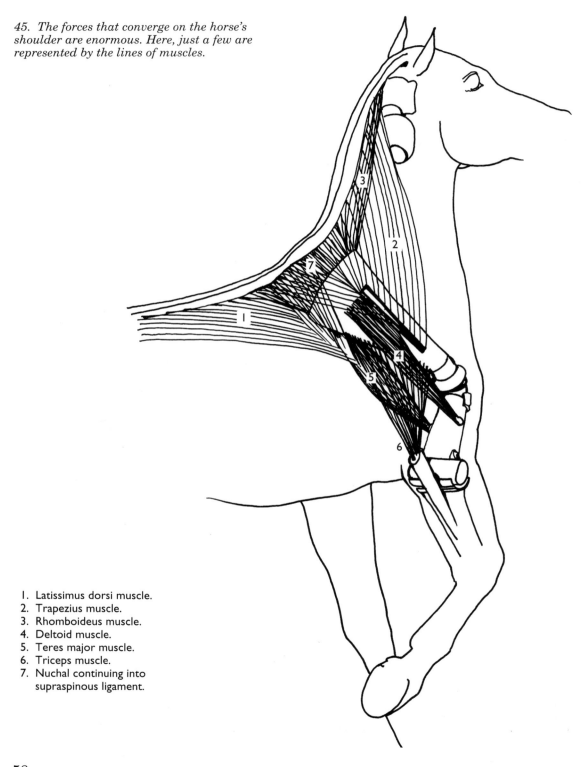

45. *The forces that converge on the horse's shoulder are enormous. Here, just a few are represented by the lines of muscles.*

1. Latissimus dorsi muscle.
2. Trapezius muscle.
3. Rhomboideus muscle.
4. Deltoid muscle.
5. Teres major muscle.
6. Triceps muscle.
7. Nuchal continuing into supraspinous ligament.

46. Muscles that move the forelimb forwards.

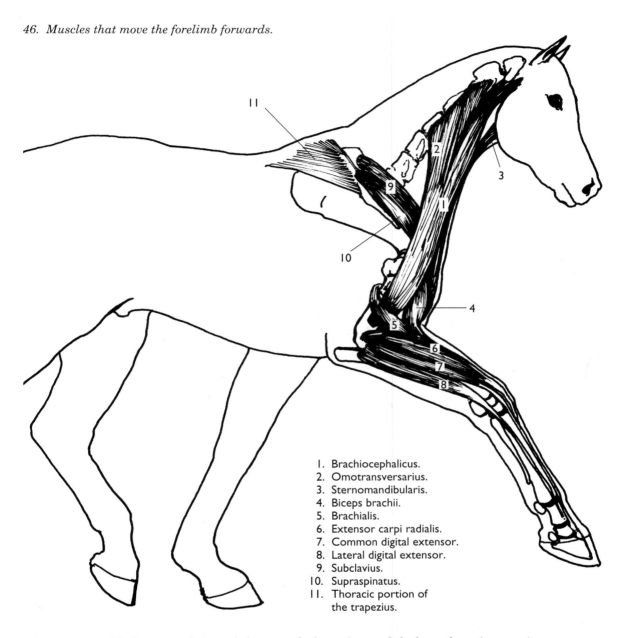

1. Brachiocephalicus.
2. Omotransversarius.
3. Sternomandibularis.
4. Biceps brachii.
5. Brachialis.
6. Extensor carpi radialis.
7. Common digital extensor.
8. Lateral digital extensor.
9. Subclavius.
10. Supraspinatus.
11. Thoracic portion of
    the trapezius.

The sternomandibularis muscle extends between the lower jaw and the breastbone (sternum). It forms the lower contour of the jugular groove. The subclavius muscle attaches to the front of the scapula, and passes over the apex of the shoulder joint to insert along the cartilage junctions of the first four ribs. Both these muscles give stability to the forehand. In riding they are used as postural muscles.

The trapezius muscle consists of two triangular portions, which extend along the 'top line' from both sides of the scapula and attach either side of the scapula spine. The combined action of both parts contributes to the pendulum swing of the foreleg. Only the thoracic part is shown here.

47. Muscles that move the forelimb backwards.

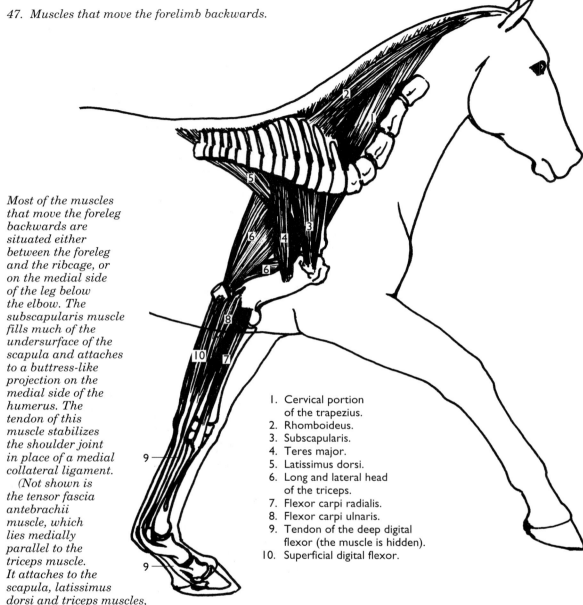

Most of the muscles that move the foreleg backwards are situated either between the foreleg and the ribcage, or on the medial side of the leg below the elbow. The subscapularis muscle fills much of the undersurface of the scapula and attaches to a buttress-like projection on the medial side of the humerus. The tendon of this muscle stabilizes the shoulder joint in place of a medial collateral ligament.

(Not shown is the tensor fascia antebrachii muscle, which lies medially parallel to the triceps muscle. It attaches to the scapula, latissimus dorsi and triceps muscles,

1. Cervical portion of the trapezius.
2. Rhomboideus.
3. Subscapularis.
4. Teres major.
5. Latissimus dorsi.
6. Long and lateral head of the triceps.
7. Flexor carpi radialis.
8. Flexor carpi ulnaris.
9. Tendon of the deep digital flexor (the muscle is hidden).
10. Superficial digital flexor.

and inserts on the olecranon process. It reinforces the effect of the other two muscles.)

The origin of the rhomboideus muscle is at the top of the nuchal ligament (not shown in this picture). It inserts under the top edge of the scapula. Its action is to pull the top of the scapula forwards, thereby allowing the foreleg to move backwards.

The cervical part of the trapezius muscle thinly covers the rhomboideus muscle on the outside of the neck. It connects the length of the nuchal ligament with the omotransversarius muscle and the scapula spine. The action of the cervical trapezius muscle depends on the posture of the horse. It should rotate the scapula forwards, but when the muscles of the lower neck are fixed it reinforces the action of the rhomboideus muscle instead. The consequence of incorrect use is to produce large unsightly lumps of hardened muscle in front of the withers.

48. *The suspension of the forehand.*

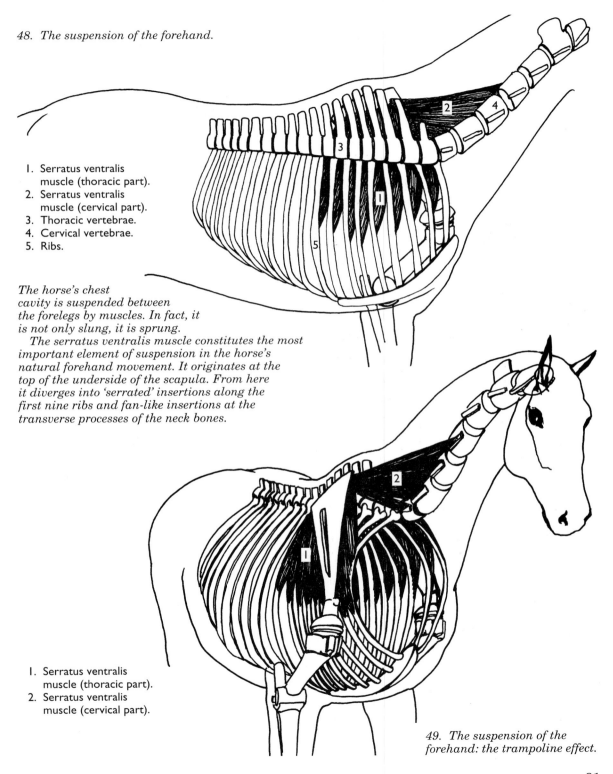

1. Serratus ventralis
   muscle (thoracic part).
2. Serratus ventralis
   muscle (cervical part).
3. Thoracic vertebrae.
4. Cervical vertebrae.
5. Ribs.

*The horse's chest
cavity is suspended between
the forelegs by muscles. In fact, it
is not only slung, it is sprung.*
   *The serratus ventralis muscle constitutes the most
important element of suspension in the horse's
natural forehand movement. It originates at the
top of the underside of the scapula. From here
it diverges into 'serrated' insertions along the
first nine ribs and fan-like insertions at the
transverse processes of the neck bones.*

1. Serratus ventralis
   muscle (thoracic part).
2. Serratus ventralis
   muscle (cervical part).

49. *The suspension of the
forehand: the trampoline effect.*

50. The suspension of the forehand: trampoline combined with springboard. (Viewed from inside the horse's chest.)

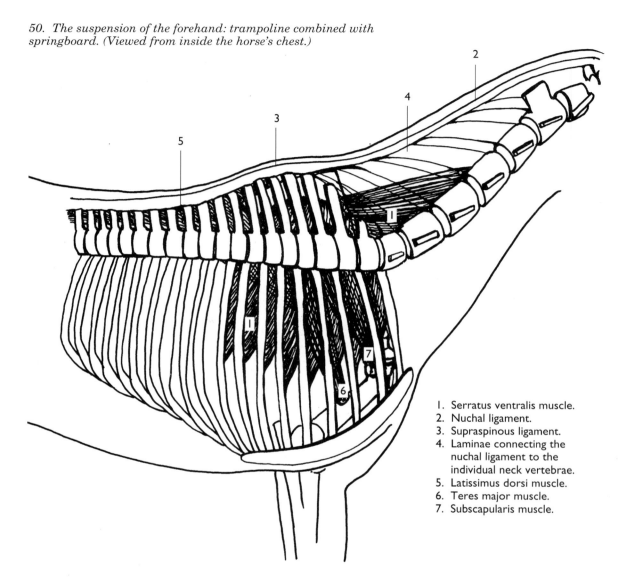

1. Serratus ventralis muscle.
2. Nuchal ligament.
3. Supraspinous ligament.
4. Laminae connecting the nuchal ligament to the individual neck vertebrae.
5. Latissimus dorsi muscle.
6. Teres major muscle.
7. Subscapularis muscle.

The serratus ventralis muscle is custom-made to elasticate the stride as the horse's limbs hit the ground. It is similar in effect to a trampoline. However, the action of the thoracic serratus ventralis muscle is combined with that of the latissimus dorsi and teres major muscles. These draw the leg back and flex the shoulder, providing a springboard from which to launch the stride into the next phase. At this moment, the shoulder joint is stabilized medially by the subscapularis muscle.

In the ridden horse, the potential of these muscles to energize the forward stride, and at the same time protect the body from the energy of impact, depends on the elasticity of the whole forehand – for example, the suppleness of the neck muscles and the traction of the nuchal and supraspinous ligaments.

If the serratus ventralis muscles is bruised by the pressure of the girth straps, or the neck is fixed by the rider's hands (or draw reins!) the whole system is rendered useless. The horse's chest cavity is mercilessly jarred with every stride.

51. The muscular sling.

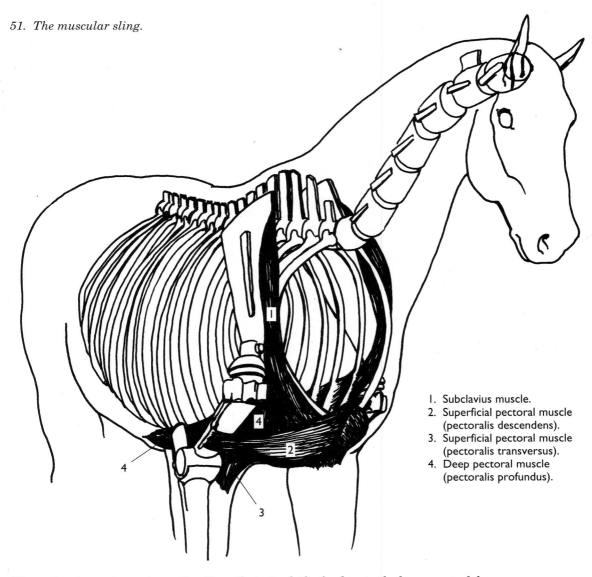

1. Subclavius muscle.
2. Superficial pectoral muscle (pectoralis descendens).
3. Superficial pectoral muscle (pectoralis transversus).
4. Deep pectoral muscle (pectoralis profundus).

The pectoral muscles make up the slings that attach the forelegs to the lower part of the ribcage. Whereas the serratus ventralis muscle (thoracic part) braces the chest for take-off, the pectoral muscles cushion it on impact.

The superficial pectoral muscle connects the sternum to the humerus and fascia of the forearm. The deep pectoral muscle connects the rear part of the sternum with the medial side of the humerus, and, via the subclavius muscle, with the top of the scapula.

The significance of the pectoral muscles in protecting the horse on landing after a jump is clear. However, the deep pectoral muscle also has the role of helping to draw the leg and shoulder backwards. It reinforces the action of the latissimus dorsi muscle. In horses that have lost the suppleness of their back or neck muscles, the pectoralis profundus muscle becomes tense, and painful. Such horses often resent being girthed up.

(In some anatomy books, the subclavius muscle is named as a continuation of the pectoralis profundus muscle.)

63

52. The suspension of the forehand in action.

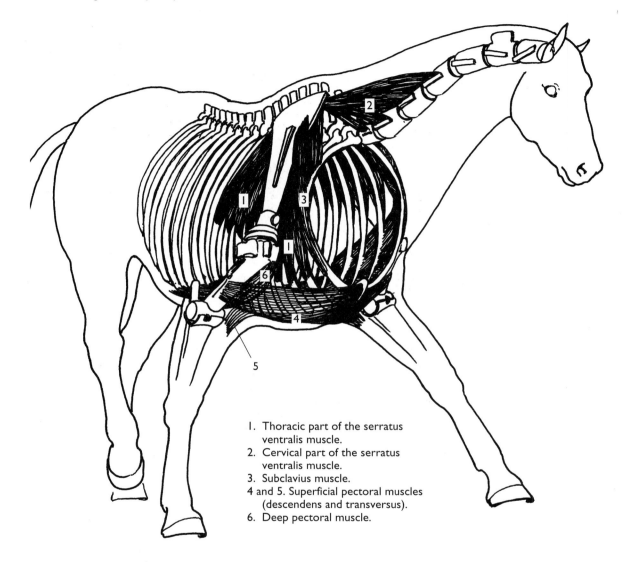

1. Thoracic part of the serratus
   ventralis muscle.
2. Cervical part of the serratus
   ventralis muscle.
3. Subclavius muscle.
4 and 5. Superficial pectoral muscles
   (descendens and transversus).
6. Deep pectoral muscle.

During one stride, the limb passes through a swing phase and a stance phase. At the trot, the change from one diagonal stride to the other makes particular demands on the horse's natural suspension.

N.B. All the muscles are bilateral, though the cervical part of the serratus ventralis cannot be seen from this angle. The aperture of the ribcage has been expanded to allow the viewer to see the serratus ventralis and deep pectoral muscles on the far side.

53. The suspension of the forehand during the swing and stance phase in conjunction with muscles that lengthen the stride.

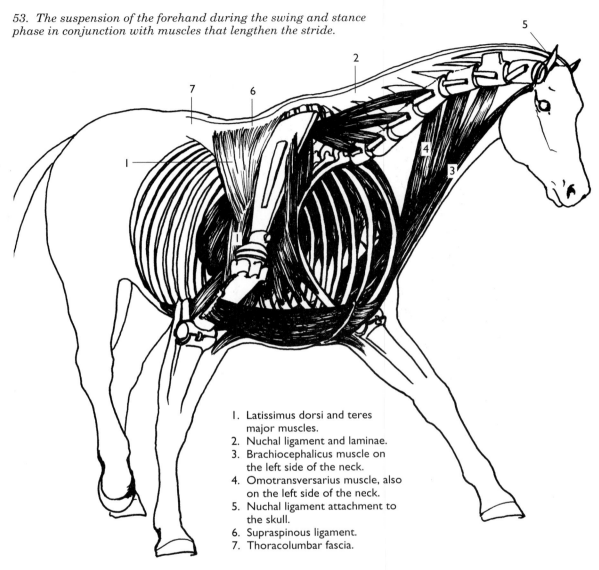

1. Latissimus dorsi and teres major muscles.
2. Nuchal ligament and laminae.
3. Brachiocephalicus muscle on the left side of the neck.
4. Omotransversarius muscle, also on the left side of the neck.
5. Nuchal ligament attachment to the skull.
6. Supraspinous ligament.
7. Thoracolumbar fascia.

The latissimus dorsi muscle inserts on the teres major muscle, and together they pull the limb backwards (retraction). The brachiocephalicus and omotransversarius muscles draw the limb forwards (protraction), but only relative to the position of the head. The height of the head-carriage is therefore a key factor in producing a specific length of stride. Not only does it enhance or restrict the action of the lower neck muscles, it also increases or reduces traction along the nuchal ligament. The laminae of the nuchal ligament stabilize the position of the neck bones, and this stability is transferred via the supraspinous ligament along the spine to the thoracolumbar fascia. This is the point of origin for the latissimus dorsi muscle.

In order to protect the forehand from jarring, the muscles of suspension have to comply with the movements of the limbs in both the swing and stance phases of the stride.

N.B. Once again, the aperture of the chest cavity has been widened to allow a view through to the other side.

54. Areas of tension and soreness that develop when the suspension is used incorrectly, or not used at all.

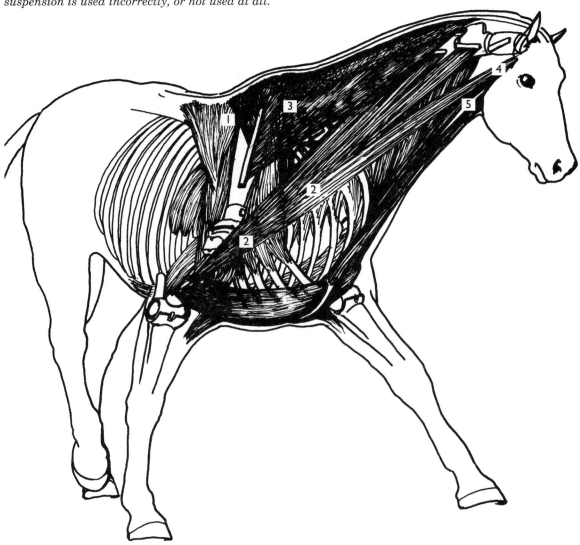

1. The rear border of the scapula where the latissimus dorsi, trapezius, and teres major muscle intersect. This place is directly under the tree of the saddle, and often under the reinforcing plates of the arch.
2. In the brachiocephalicus muscle, in front of the shoulder joint or at the base of the neck just above the jugular groove.
3. In front of the withers, where the trapezius and rhomboideus muscles overlap.
4. In the brachiocephalicus muscle, between the wing of the atlas and the jawline.
5. In the sternomandibularis muscle below the line of the bottom jaw.

N.B. Again, the aperture of the chest has been widened.

55. The purpose of the thorax.

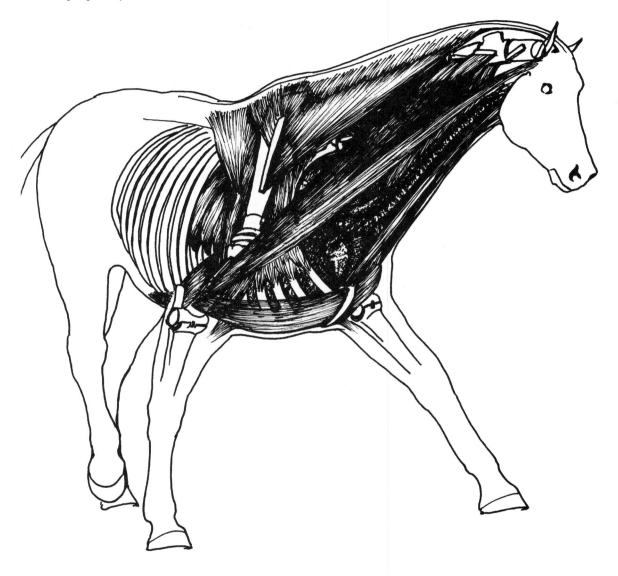

Despite its apparent suitability for the task, the horse's chest is not built for the sole purpose of bearing the weight of a saddle. It houses vital organs, namely the heart and lungs. Although the inherent strength of the ribcage makes it adaptable to carrying the rider's weight, the muscles of suspension should never be compromised.

N.B. In reality, the passage into the chest cavity is much narrower, allowing just enough room for the gullet, windpipe, jugular veins and carotid arteries.

56. The suspension muscles are particularly important when one is eating!

1. Thoracic part of the serratus ventralis muscle.
2. Cervical part of the serratus ventralis muscle.
3. Subclavius muscle.
4. Superficial pectoral muscles.
5. Deep pectoral muscle.

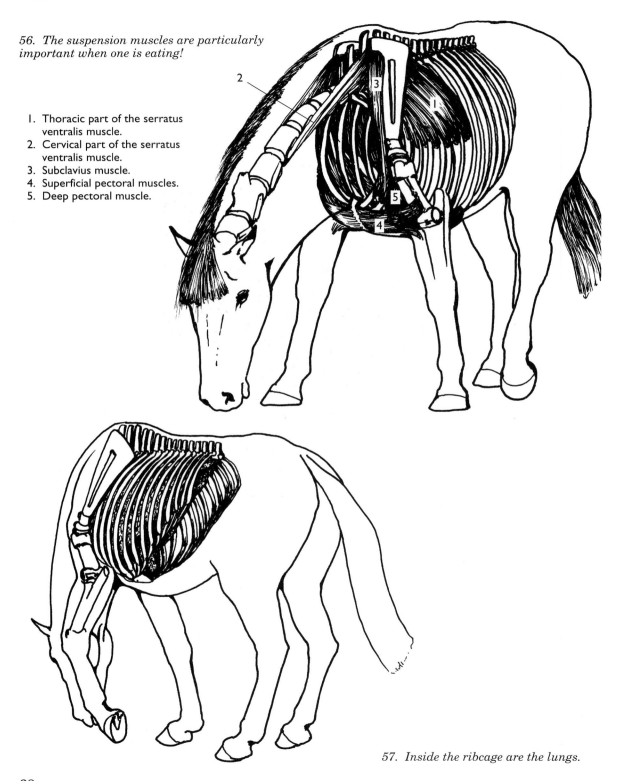

57. Inside the ribcage are the lungs.

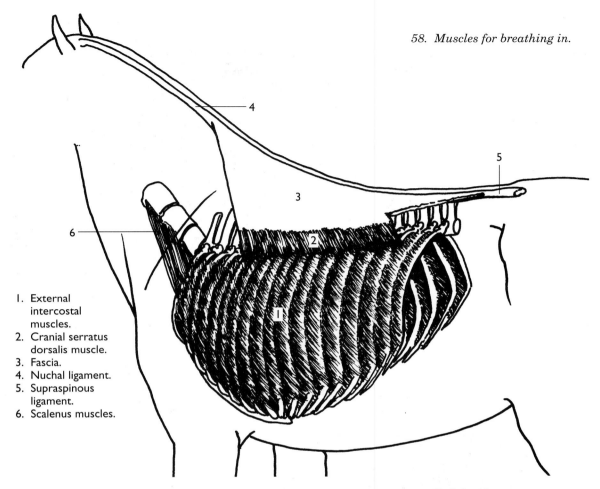

58. Muscles for breathing in.

1. External intercostal muscles.
2. Cranial serratus dorsalis muscle.
3. Fascia.
4. Nuchal ligament.
5. Supraspinous ligament.
6. Scalenus muscles.

The lungs and the inner wall of the chest are covered by a thin layer of tissue called the pleura. Although the two surfaces are moist, and can slip past one another without abrasion, there is virtually no space in between. Therefore, when the ribcage expands, the passages in the lungs are opened, allowing the air to enter. When the ribcage contracts, the natural elasticity of the lung tissue squeezes the air out again.

The heads of the ribs have twofold articulations with the vertebrae of the thoracic spine; these allow the ribs to rotate forwards. Only the first nine ribs are secured by cartilage to the sternum. The remaining nine ribs have cartilage elongations that attach to each other to form the line of a continuous arc.

Breathing in (inspiration) and breathing out (expiration) are controlled mainly by the direction of the muscles that lie between the ribs.

The external intercostal muscles slope backwards and downwards (caudoventrally). When they contract, the ribs are pulled forwards and outwards, opening the ribcage (sometimes from as far back as the hindmost rib). Since the first six ribs lie under the muscles of the foreleg, there is not much room for movement here. Two small muscles, the scalenus medius and scalenus ventralis, attach to the first rib and insert at the lowest neck vertebrae. They act only on the first rib. The action of the external intercostal muscles is assisted by the front (cranial) portion of the serratus dorsalis muscle, which originates in a broad band of connective tissue, linking the muscle indirectly to the nuchal and supraspinous ligaments.

We should remember that all these muscles lie immediately under the saddle and may be compromised by saddle pressure and by the leg and seat aids of the rider.

59. *Muscles for breathing out.*

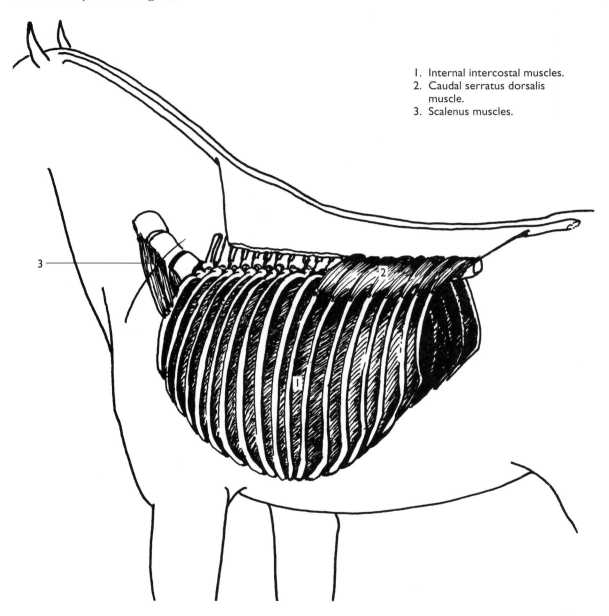

1. Internal intercostal muscles.
2. Caudal serratus dorsalis muscle.
3. Scalenus muscles.

The inner layer of intercostal muscles lies at right angles to the outer layer. These muscles slope forwards and downwards. When they contract the ribcage is closed, starting with the hindmost rib. The rear portion of the serratus dorsalis muscle assists by acting on the tops of the last ribs.

The position of the scalenus muscle is included, not because it contributes to expiration but because, as will be seen later, the first rib lies at a very vulnerable junction of the spine.

*60. The most important breathing muscle of
all: the diaphragm.*

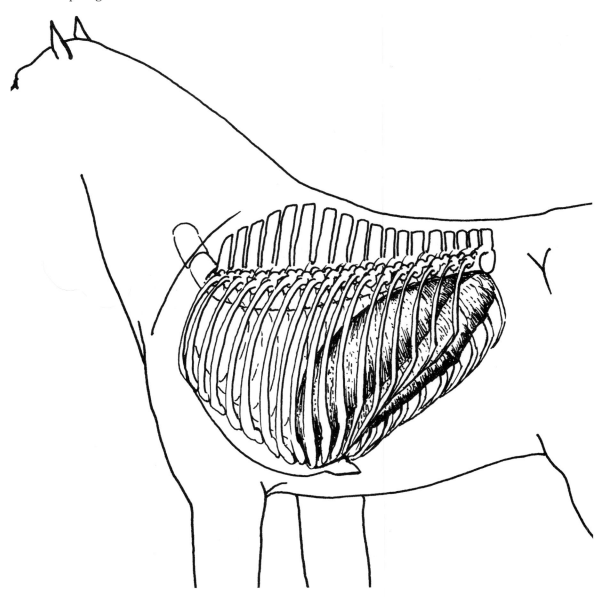

*The diaphragm is attached to the inside of the chest wall. It resembles an umbrella, which
opens and shuts as the ribcage expands and contracts with the action of the intercostal muscles.*

*Although the preceding descriptions of the breathing mechanism have assumed that the
horse is breathing deeply, of course he does not need to do this the whole time. In fact, at rest,
the movement of the entire ribcage should be virtually imperceptible.*

*However, it can be seen from the position of the diaphragm that the rider is likely to
influence this physiologically very important structure.*

61. Lifting the abdomen.

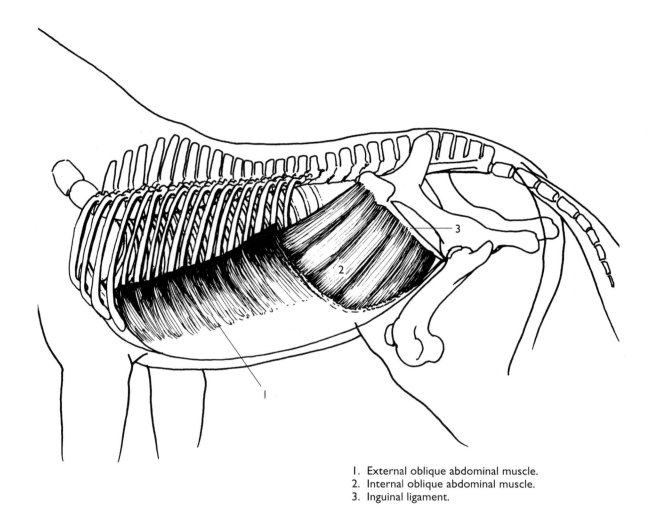

1. External oblique abdominal muscle.
2. Internal oblique abdominal muscle.
3. Inguinal ligament.

Although the abdominal muscles do not produce locomotion, they make a vital contribution to the stability of the spinal column. If we imagine that the spine represents a bow, and the line of the abdomen the bowstring, it is clear that both need to be in traction before the body can be adequately supported during movement. After all, the abdomen contains the enormous fermentation chambers of the horse's gut.

The direction of muscle fibres in the external and internal oblique abdominal muscles continue the direction of those in the external and internal intercostal muscles.

62. Lifting the abdomen.

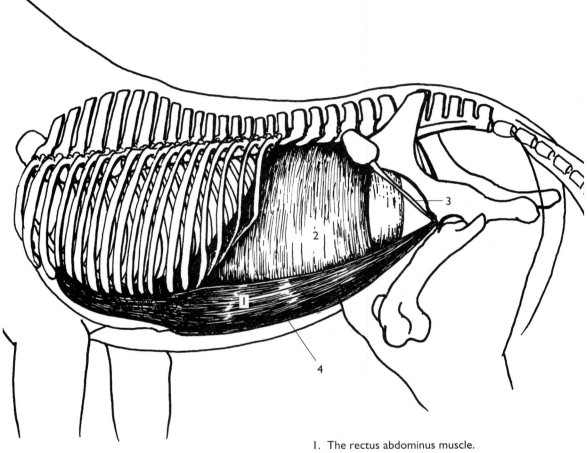

1. The rectus abdominus muscle.
2. The transverse abdominal muscle.
3. Inguinal ligament.
4. Linea alba.

Whereas the ribcage is adequately reinforced by the ribs, the abdomen is supported by extra layers of muscle. This allows for the fluctuating amount of the gut contents and for pregnancy.

Strictly speaking, the 'bowstring' is formed by the rectus abdominis muscle and by the linea alba, which is a strong line of connective tissue between the abdominal muscles of both sides. However, the action of the abdominal muscles is linked by their specific nervous supply so that in effect they all contribute to the support of the horse's belly.

The rectus abdominis muscle continues forward as far as the cartilages of the ninth to fourth ribs. These are also the places of insertion for the deep pectoral muscle.

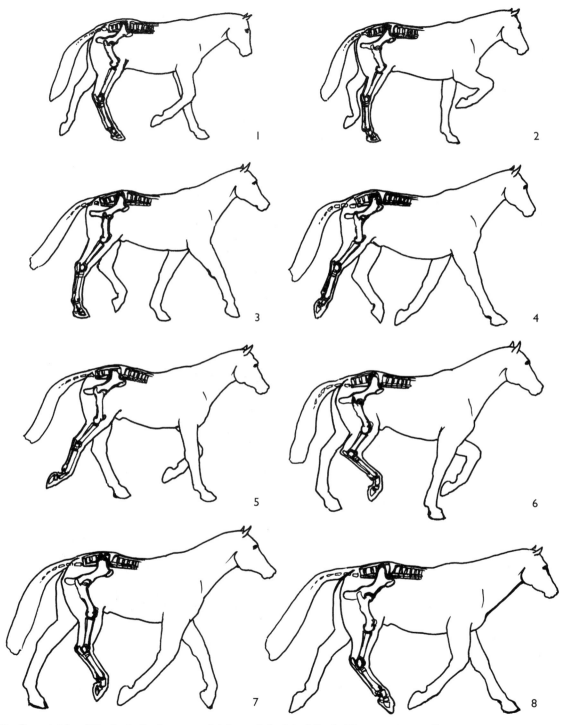

63. One stride of the trot: the bones and joints of the hind limb. Pictures 1 to 8 illustrate the stance and swing phases of a stride completed by the right hind limb.

64. *One stride of the trot: the changing emphasis of muscle movement. Pictures 1 to 8 illustrate the action of the hind-limb muscles during the stance and swing phases of a stride. Note the shift of weight to the inside thigh muscles of the left hind leg in pictures 6 and 7.*

65. The joints of the forelimb (A) and hind limb (B).

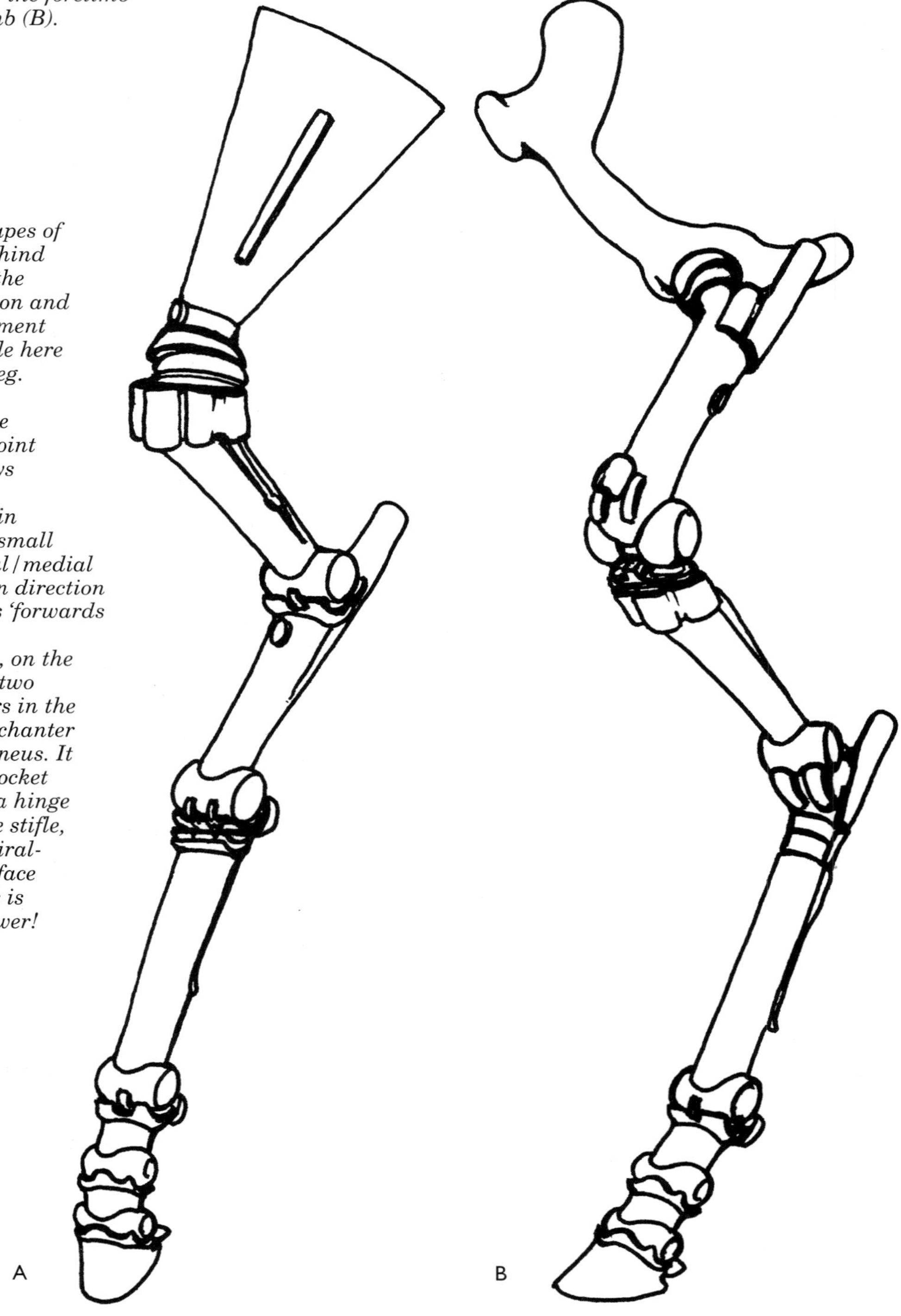

Compare the shapes of the joints in the hind limb to those of the forelimb. Direction and breadth of movement are more versatile here than in the foreleg.

Although the horizontal sphere of the shoulder joint allows a sideways twist, and the pastern and coffin joints tolerate a small amount of lateral / medial tipping, the main direction of the forelimb is 'forwards and onwards'.

The hind limb, on the other hand, has two substantial levers in the shapes of the trochanter major and calcaneus. It has a ball-and-socket joint at the hip, a hinge and pulley at the stifle, and a further spiral-shaped joint surface at the hock. This is steering with power!

A

B

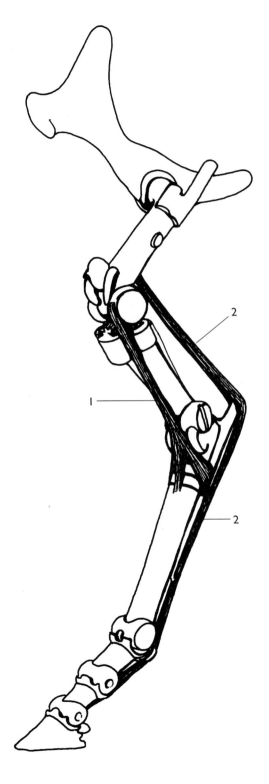

It is hardly possible to understand the movement of the hind limb without recognizing the importance of the so-called reciprocal apparatus. This mechanism consists of two fundamental structures, although it is assisted by other muscles in the vicinity.

The peroneus tertius muscle is not a muscle but a tendon that originates at the stifle joint just in front of, and above, the large condyle of the femur. At the opposite end, it divides into three and inserts: on the inside of the cannon bone; on the central and third tarsal bones, and at the top of the cannon bone; and, after passing under the trochlea of the talus, on the fourth tarsal bone.

The superficial digital flexor muscle contains some muscle fibres but it, too, is largely a tendon. It originates in a hollow between the two condyles at the back of the femur. It attaches to the calcaneus (point of the hock), and becomes the superficial digital flexor tendon. This inserts at the back of the short pastern bone, just as it does in the forelimb.

The presence of these two structures means that whatever angle the stifle makes, the hock has to imitate it. For example, if the hinge of the stifle closes, the peroneus tertius closes the angle of the hock. If the hinge of the stifle opens, the superficial digital flexor opens the angle of the hock.

Not only are the hock and stifle inextricably linked to their action, but the fetlock joint is also connected to the mechanism. It automatically adopts the correct position for whatever the stifle and hock are about to do.

1. Peroneus tertius 'muscle' (also called fibularis tertius).
2. Superficial digital flexor muscle, and tendon.

66. The reciprocal apparatus of the hind limb.

67. Connecting the stifle mechanism to the reciprocal apparatus.

1. Quadriceps femoris muscle.
2. Peroneus tertius 'muscle'.
3. Superficial digital flexor muscle.
4. Superficial digital flexor tendon.

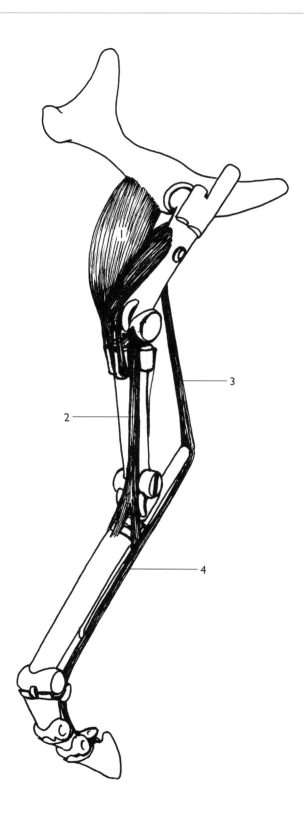

The mechanical efficiency of the hind leg does not end with the reciprocal apparatus. The stifle has its own ingenious device in the shape of the patella. The patella is moved in the groove between the pulley-like wheels of the (femoral) trochlea by the action of the quadriceps femoris muscle. This muscle (whose name literally means four heads) consists of four smaller muscles: the rectus femoris, the vastus lateralis, the vastus medius, and the vastus intermedius. The rectus femoris muscle begins at the pelvis, the other three at the top of the femur. The muscles combine above the stifle and insert on the tibia, feeding into the middle patellar ligament.

The action of the quadriceps femoris muscle is to extend the stifle (femorotibial) joint. In doing this, it automatically engages the reciprocal apparatus.

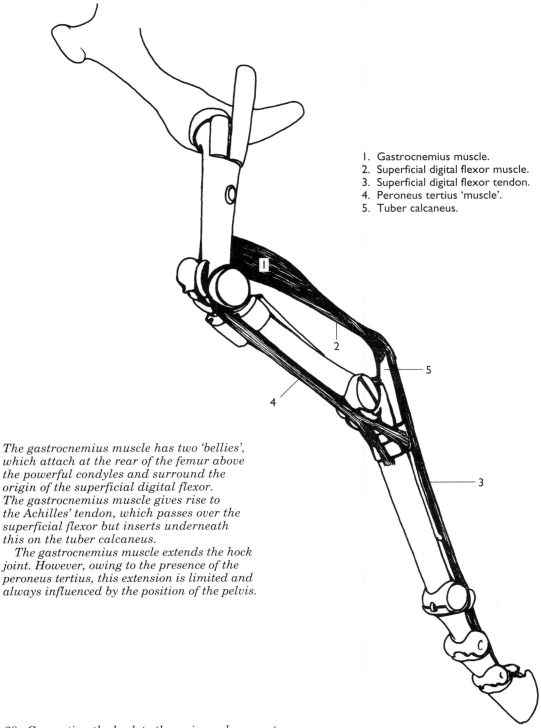

1. Gastrocnemius muscle.
2. Superficial digital flexor muscle.
3. Superficial digital flexor tendon.
4. Peroneus tertius 'muscle'.
5. Tuber calcaneus.

*The gastrocnemius muscle has two 'bellies',
which attach at the rear of the femur above
the powerful condyles and surround the
origin of the superficial digital flexor.
The gastrocnemius muscle gives rise to
the Achilles' tendon, which passes over the
superficial flexor but inserts underneath
this on the tuber calcaneus.*

*The gastrocnemius muscle extends the hock
joint. However, owing to the presence of the
peroneus tertius, this extension is limited and
always influenced by the position of the pelvis.*

68. *Connecting the hock to the reciprocal apparatus.*

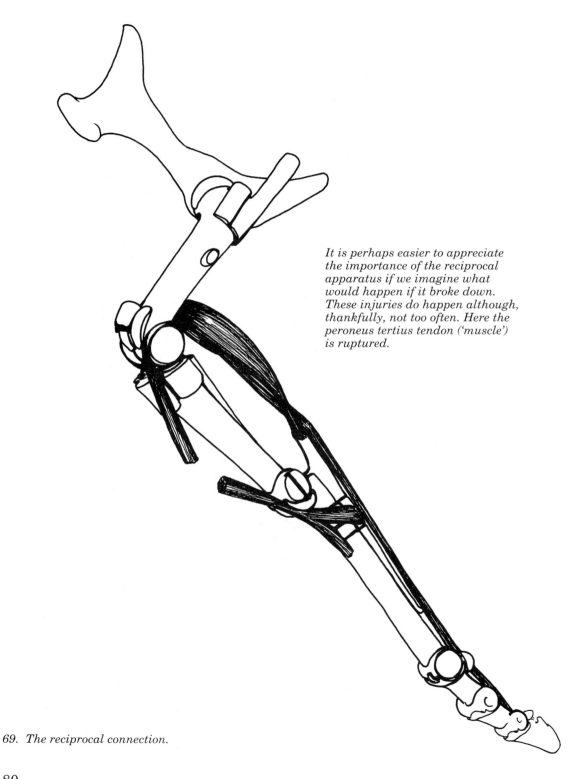

It is perhaps easier to appreciate the importance of the reciprocal apparatus if we imagine what would happen if it broke down. These injuries do happen although, thankfully, not too often. Here the peroneus tertius tendon ('muscle') is ruptured.

69. The reciprocal connection.

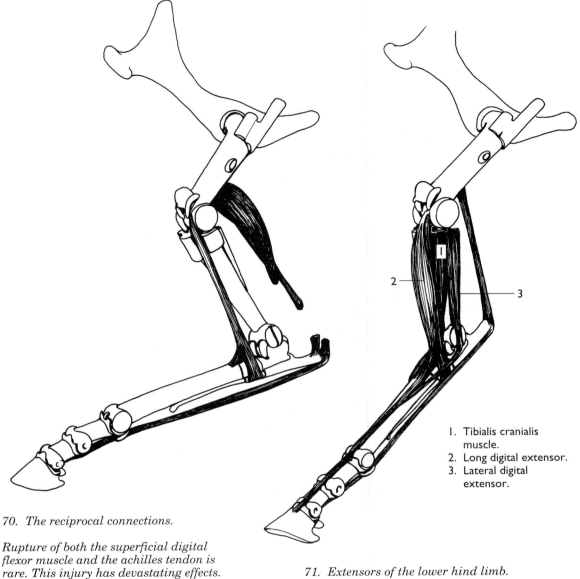

70. The reciprocal connections.

Rupture of both the superficial digital flexor muscle and the achilles tendon is rare. This injury has devastating effects.

1. Tibialis cranialis muscle.
2. Long digital extensor.
3. Lateral digital extensor.

71. Extensors of the lower hind limb.

The long digital extensors are like those of the forelimb, although the terminology used to describe them is slightly different. The two insertions of the short extensor muscle (the tibialis cranialis) add to the complex organization of the threefold insertions of the peroneus tertius. The small bones of the hock joint are criss-crossed by a network of ligaments and their retaining straps of connective tissue.

The tendon of the lateral digital extensor lies in its own groove at the bottom end of the tibia.

81

72. *The deep digital flexor muscle and tendon.*

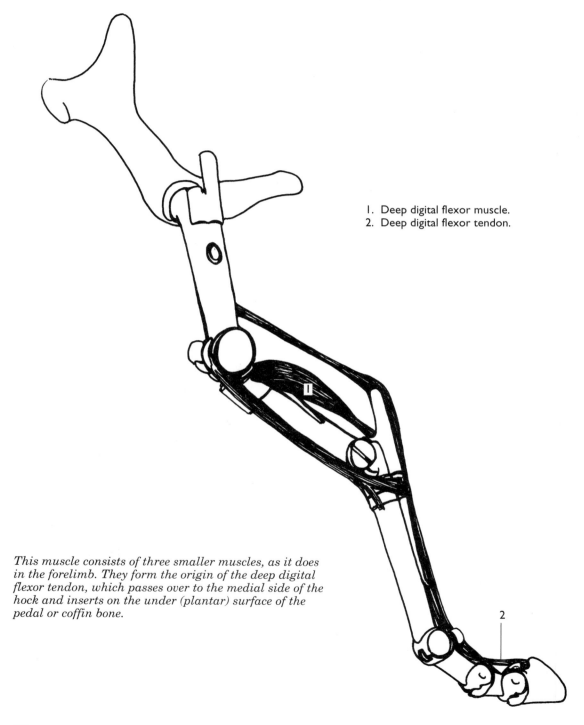

1. Deep digital flexor muscle.
2. Deep digital flexor tendon.

This muscle consists of three smaller muscles, as it does in the forelimb. They form the origin of the deep digital flexor tendon, which passes over to the medial side of the hock and inserts on the under (plantar) surface of the pedal or coffin bone.

Like the tendons of the foreleg, the tendons of the hind leg need to be anchored at the major points of articulation.

In this illustration, only the strap-like attachments at the front of the hock are shown. The superficial flexor tendon and the tendon of the gastrocnemius muscle (Achilles' tendon) attach directly to the calcaneus. (The arrangement at the fetlock and foot is the same as for the forelimb.) The purpose of these 'straps' is clear if we consider the range of movement in the hock. However, the tendons are held close to an already dense web of ligaments that prevent the small hock bones from moving while the main joint surface of the talus rotates against the tibia.

Where it passes underneath a strap (retinaculum), each tendon is enclosed in a lubricated sheath of connective tissue. Nevertheless, friction does occur, particularly if the joint itself cannot move freely. This happens when the hind leg is incorrectly engaged, or not engaged at all. (N.B. The tendon of the lateral digital extensor muscle has its own groove on the side of the lower tibia, and is not anchored to the skeleton until it joins the digital extensor.)

The whole body is swathed in broad expanses of 'fascia' – connective tissue that contains a mesh of collagen and elastic fibres. This mesh gives the fascia high tensile strength. In most places throughout the body, the presence of fascia protects the layers of muscles and ensures that their surfaces glide past each other without interference. When fascia becomes damaged through injury or infection, scar tissue develops, which effectively glues individual muscles together. These areas are called adhesions.

In the hind limb, the structure of the fascia plays an integral part in movement. The hind limb fascia consists of several layers. The superficial layer encloses the whole musculature. The deeper layers wrap around individual muscles. However, the fascia has fibrous attachments to bone surfaces and ligaments, and, most importantly, serves as a place of insertion for the powerful muscles of the hindquarters.

Unlike those of the upper forelimb, many muscles of the upper hind limb do not attach directly to the bones. They use the fascia. In other words, the muscles pull on the fascia and the fascia pulls on the joint. This action is especially relevant to the stifle joint, where the fascia has attachments to the femur, the patella, and the three patellar ligaments.

1. Proximal extensor retinaculum.
2. Middle extensor retinaculum.
3. Distal extensor retinaculum.
4. Fascia.
5. Stifle.

73. Retaining structures of the hind limb.

83

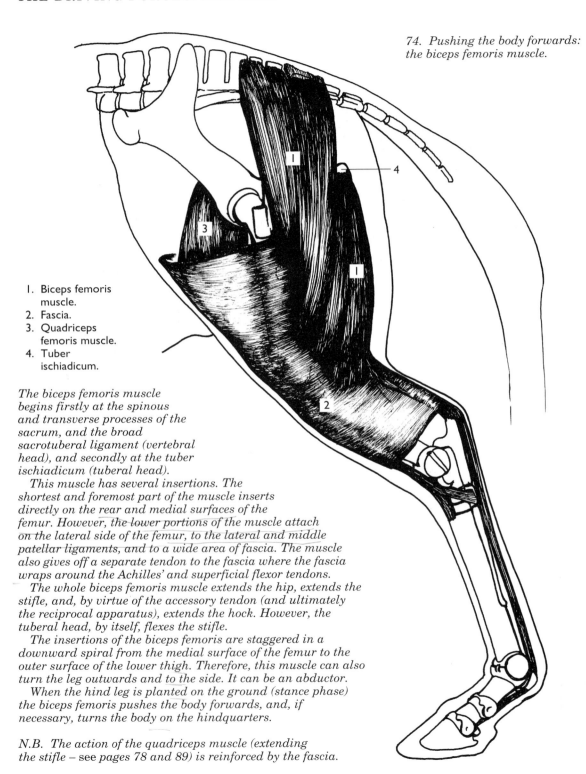

74. *Pushing the body forwards:*
the biceps femoris muscle.

1. Biceps femoris
   muscle.
2. Fascia.
3. Quadriceps
   femoris muscle.
4. Tuber
   ischiadicum.

The biceps femoris muscle
begins firstly at the spinous
and transverse processes of the
sacrum, and the broad
sacrotuberal ligament (vertebral
head), and secondly at the tuber
ischiadicum (tuberal head).
  This muscle has several insertions. The
shortest and foremost part of the muscle inserts
directly on the rear and medial surfaces of the
femur. However, the lower portions of the muscle attach
on the lateral side of the femur, to the lateral and middle
patellar ligaments, and to a wide area of fascia. The muscle
also gives off a separate tendon to the fascia where the fascia
wraps around the Achilles' and superficial flexor tendons.
  The whole biceps femoris muscle extends the hip, extends the
stifle, and, by virtue of the accessory tendon (and ultimately
the reciprocal apparatus), extends the hock. However, the
tuberal head, by itself, flexes the stifle.
  The insertions of the biceps femoris are staggered in a
downward spiral from the medial surface of the femur to the
outer surface of the lower thigh. Therefore, this muscle can also
turn the leg outwards and to the side. It can be an abductor.
  When the hind leg is planted on the ground (stance phase)
the biceps femoris pushes the body forwards, and, if
necessary, turns the body on the hindquarters.

N.B. The action of the quadriceps muscle (extending
the stifle – see pages 78 and 89) is reinforced by the fascia.

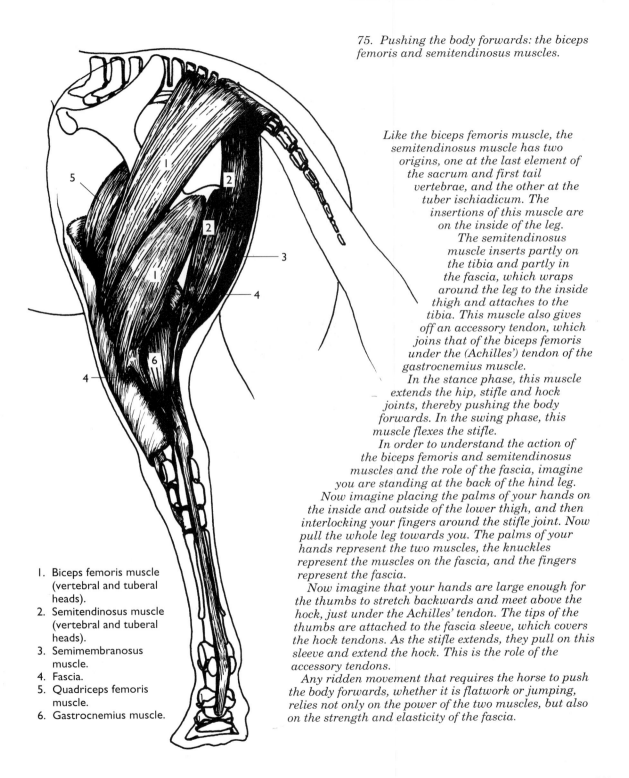

75. *Pushing the body forwards: the biceps femoris and semitendinosus muscles.*

Like the biceps femoris muscle, the semitendinosus muscle has two origins, one at the last element of the sacrum and first tail vertebrae, and the other at the tuber ischiadicum. The insertions of this muscle are on the inside of the leg. The semitendinosus muscle inserts partly on the tibia and partly in the fascia, which wraps around the leg to the inside thigh and attaches to the tibia. This muscle also gives off an accessory tendon, which joins that of the biceps femoris under the (Achilles') tendon of the gastrocnemius muscle.

In the stance phase, this muscle extends the hip, stifle and hock joints, thereby pushing the body forwards. In the swing phase, this muscle flexes the stifle.

In order to understand the action of the biceps femoris and semitendinosus muscles and the role of the fascia, imagine you are standing at the back of the hind leg. Now imagine placing the palms of your hands on the inside and outside of the lower thigh, and then interlocking your fingers around the stifle joint. Now pull the whole leg towards you. The palms of your hands represent the two muscles, the knuckles represent the muscles on the fascia, and the fingers represent the fascia.

Now imagine that your hands are large enough for the thumbs to stretch backwards and meet above the hock, just under the Achilles' tendon. The tips of the thumbs are attached to the fascia sleeve, which covers the hock tendons. As the stifle extends, they pull on this sleeve and extend the hock. This is the role of the accessory tendons.

Any ridden movement that requires the horse to push the body forwards, whether it is flatwork or jumping, relies not only on the power of the two muscles, but also on the strength and elasticity of the fascia.

1. Biceps femoris muscle (vertebral and tuberal heads).
2. Semitendinosus muscle (vertebral and tuberal heads).
3. Semimembranosus muscle.
4. Fascia.
5. Quadriceps femoris muscle.
6. Gastrocnemius muscle.

76. *Pushing the body forwards, and sometimes kicking out! The semimembranosus muscle.*

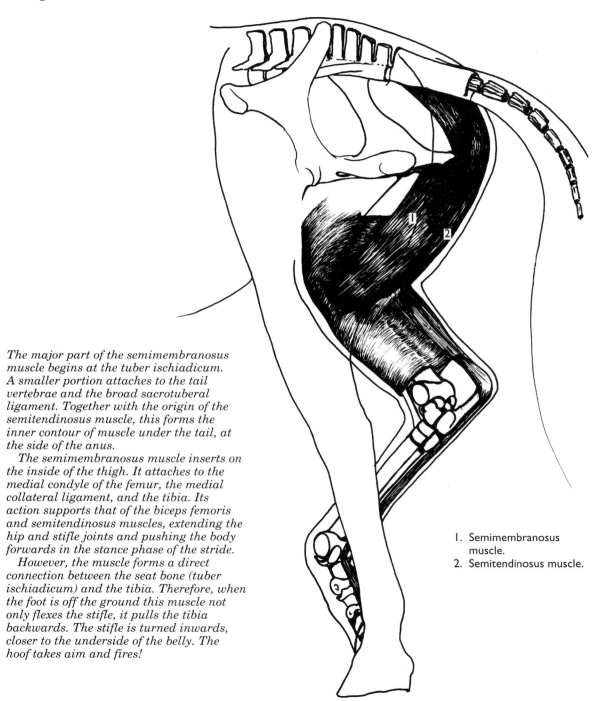

The major part of the semimembranosus muscle begins at the tuber ischiadicum. A smaller portion attaches to the tail vertebrae and the broad sacrotuberal ligament. Together with the origin of the semitendinosus muscle, this forms the inner contour of muscle under the tail, at the side of the anus.

The semimembranosus muscle inserts on the inside of the thigh. It attaches to the medial condyle of the femur, the medial collateral ligament, and the tibia. Its action supports that of the biceps femoris and semitendinosus muscles, extending the hip and stifle joints and pushing the body forwards in the stance phase of the stride.

However, the muscle forms a direct connection between the seat bone (tuber ischiadicum) and the tibia. Therefore, when the foot is off the ground this muscle not only flexes the stifle, it pulls the tibia backwards. The stifle is turned inwards, closer to the underside of the belly. The hoof takes aim and fires!

1. Semimembranosus muscle.
2. Semitendinosus muscle.

86

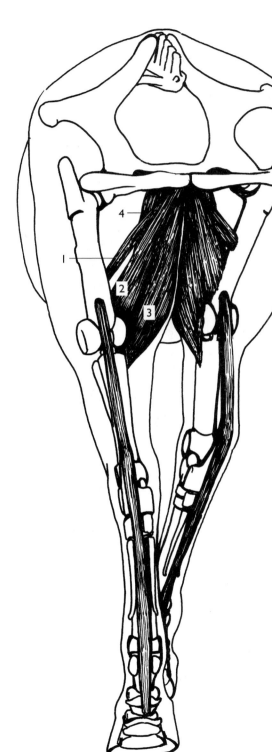

1. Pectineus muscle.
2. Adductor muscle.
3. Gracilis muscle.
4. Sartorius muscle.

In this view, the tail of the horse has been removed and the onlooker is standing to the rear of the horse.

The four muscles begin at various locations along the undersurface of the pelvis. The pectineus and adductor muscles insert on the medial side of the femur. The gracilis and sartorius muscles insert (via the fascia) on the medial patellar ligament and medial side of the tibia. They assist in the flexion of the hip and stifle joints, but their main purpose is to prevent the hind legs from splaying out. They are adductors.

77. The inner thigh muscles.

78. Small muscles of the hip joint.

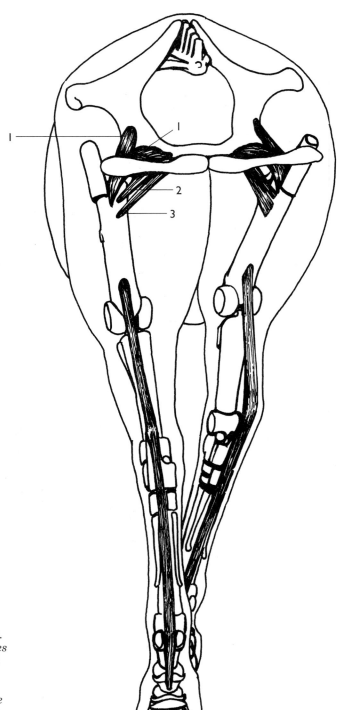

1. Internal obturatorius muscle.
2. External obturatorius muscle.
3. Quadratus femoris muscle.

The hip joint is a ball-and-socket joint. However, it is overlaid by large muscles on the outside of the pelvic girdle, and these govern the degree of rotation. Nevertheless, there is a handful of small muscles immediately around the joint, which, though not prime movers, undoubtedly become painful when the hips are out of balance.

79. *Bringing the hind leg forwards.*

1. Psoas minor muscle.
2. Iliopsoas muscle
   (psoas major).
3. Iliopsoas muscle (iliacus).
4. Quadriceps femoris muscle.
5. Diaphragm.
6. Lumbar vertebrae.

The psoas minor and iliopsoas muscles cannot be seen from the outside of the horse. Nevertheless, they are perhaps the most important muscles in the ridden horse. The successful transfer of power and lift (impulsion) from the muscles of the hindquarters depends entirely on their co-operation.

The psoas minor muscle begins inside the ribcage. Its origin covers the area of the last three ribs, including part of the diaphragm muscle, and the underside of four lumbar vertebrae. From here the muscle narrows to insert on the medial side of the ilium bone of the pelvis.

The iliopsoas muscle consists of two parts, one that begins under the lumbar vertebrae, and one that begins under the ilium and sacrum. The two parts unite, and insert on the medial side of the femur at a protuberance called the trochanter minor.

To understand the significance of the psoas group of muscles, we have to remember the action of the quadriceps femoris. The quadriceps femoris muscle (consisting of four individual muscles) inserts on the tibia and extends the stifle. This action is linked to the hock by the mechanism of the reciprocal apparatus. However, in order for the horse to bring the hock under his body, the pelvis must be lowered and the lumbar spine stabilized. This is the responsibility of the psoas minor and iliopsoas muscles.

80. Bringing the hind leg forwards.

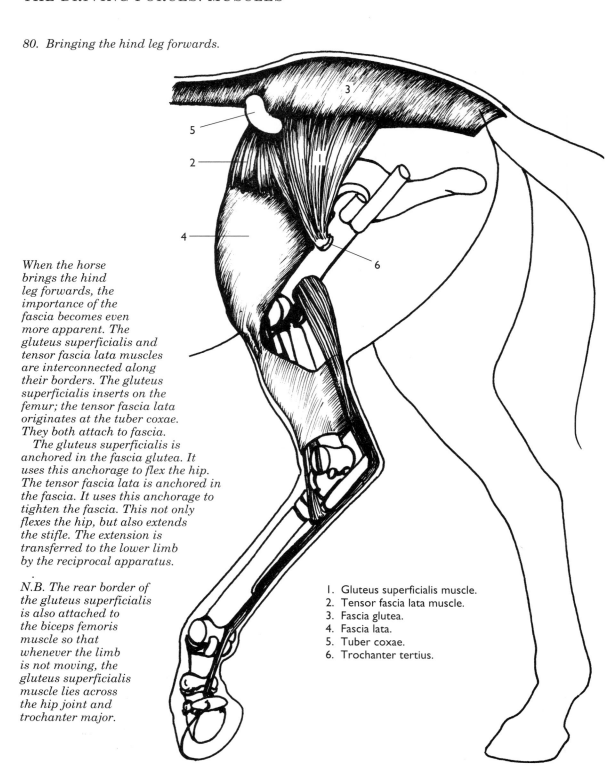

When the horse brings the hind leg forwards, the importance of the fascia becomes even more apparent. The gluteus superficialis and tensor fascia lata muscles are interconnected along their borders. The gluteus superficialis inserts on the femur; the tensor fascia lata originates at the tuber coxae. They both attach to fascia.

The gluteus superficialis is anchored in the fascia glutea. It uses this anchorage to flex the hip. The tensor fascia lata is anchored in the fascia. It uses this anchorage to tighten the fascia. This not only flexes the hip, but also extends the stifle. The extension is transferred to the lower limb by the reciprocal apparatus.

N.B. The rear border of the gluteus superficialis is also attached to the biceps femoris muscle so that whenever the limb is not moving, the gluteus superficialis muscle lies across the hip joint and trochanter major.

1. Gluteus superficialis muscle.
2. Tensor fascia lata muscle.
3. Fascia glutea.
4. Fascia lata.
5. Tuber coxae.
6. Trochanter tertius.

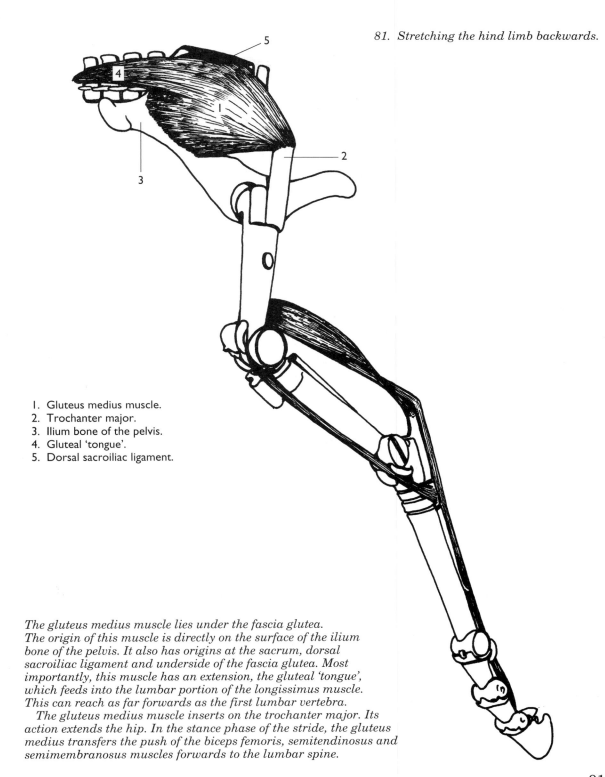

81. Stretching the hind limb backwards.

1. Gluteus medius muscle.
2. Trochanter major.
3. Ilium bone of the pelvis.
4. Gluteal 'tongue'.
5. Dorsal sacroiliac ligament.

*The gluteus medius muscle lies under the fascia glutea.
The origin of this muscle is directly on the surface of the ilium
bone of the pelvis. It also has origins at the sacrum, dorsal
sacroiliac ligament and underside of the fascia glutea. Most
importantly, this muscle has an extension, the gluteal 'tongue',
which feeds into the lumbar portion of the longissimus muscle.
This can reach as far forwards as the first lumbar vertebra.*

*The gluteus medius muscle inserts on the trochanter major. Its
action extends the hip. In the stance phase of the stride, the gluteus
medius transfers the push of the biceps femoris, semitendinosus and
semimembranosus muscles forwards to the lumbar spine.*

82. The powerful origin of impulsion.

The action of every joint
in the horse's hind limb is
linked to the action of another
joint by a muscle, a tendon, or
part of the fascia.

However, whereas the hip joint
simply passes from flexion to
extension in the course of one stride,
the stifle and lower joints variously
flex and extend. This allows the foot
to clear the ground as the limb moves
forwards, but push off from the ground
as the limb is drawn backwards.

In the unridden and untrained horse,
the natural muscle bulk favours the
gluteus medius and biceps femoris
muscles. They have the power to propel
the body forwards, and the suspension of
the chest muscles protects the forehand
from concussion.

In horses that are ridden, the chest muscles
alone do not have the capacity to suspend the
forehand when it is combined with the rider's
weight. The contribution of the tensor fascia
lata, gluteus superficialis, and quadriceps
femoris muscles becomes vital.

The gluteus superficialis and tensor
fascia lata muscles are used to flex
the hip. This flexion first tightens
the passive support for the stifle
joint through the fascia. In
turn, the fascia reinforces the
action of the quadriceps muscle
as it begins to extend the stifle.
The extension of the stifle, and
the whole limb, is then taken
over by the biceps femoris,
semitendinosus and
semimembranosus muscles.

By increasing the flexion of the
hip and the stability of the stifle –
and consequently the extension of the
stifle – it is possible to use the natural
facility of the horse to take more weight on
the hindquarters. If he is strong enough in
the back, he will be able to lift the rider, and
protect his forehand.

Poor development of those muscles that fill the triangle between the pelvis, femur and
line of the flank (tensor fascia lata, and quadriceps femoris), always means poor
impulsion. It usually goes hand in hand with stifle wear or back pain.

1. Gluteus medius muscle.
2. Gluteal 'tongue'.
3. Biceps femoris muscle.
4. Semitendinosus muscle.
5. Semimembranosus muscle.
6. Accessory tendon.
7. Fascia.
8. Quadriceps femoris muscle.
9. Tensor fascia lata
   muscle (outline).

83. Assisting the gastrocnemius muscle.

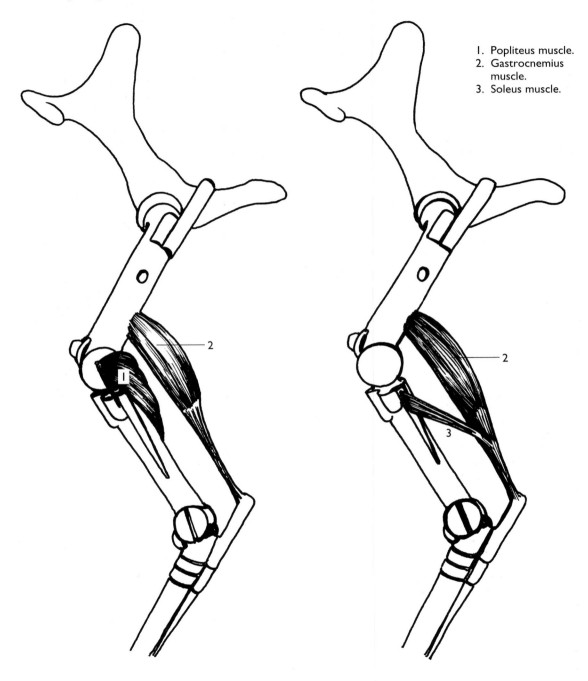

1. Popliteus muscle.
2. Gastrocnemius muscle.
3. Soleus muscle.

There are two small muscles to the rear of the stifle joint: the popliteus muscle has a minor role in flexing the stifle; the soleus muscle has a minor role in extending the hock.

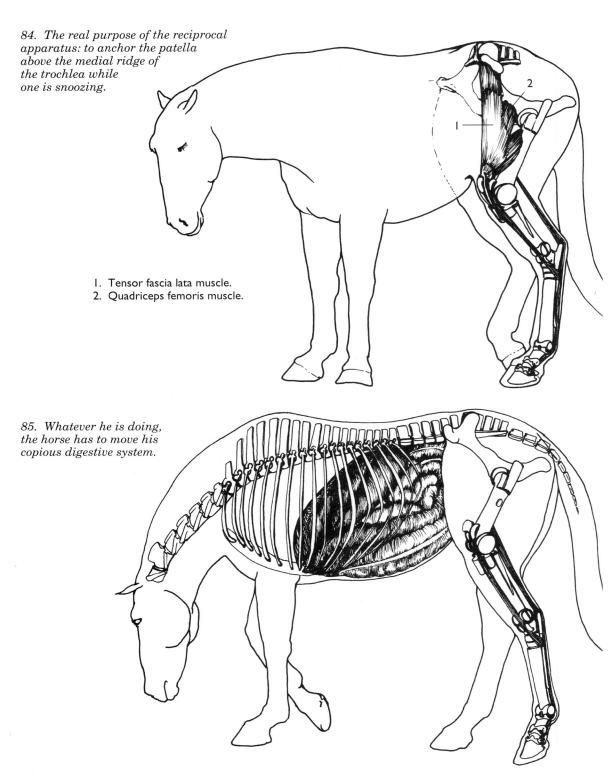

84. The real purpose of the reciprocal apparatus: to anchor the patella above the medial ridge of the trochlea while one is snoozing.

1. Tensor fascia lata muscle.
2. Quadriceps femoris muscle.

85. Whatever he is doing, the horse has to move his copious digestive system.

94

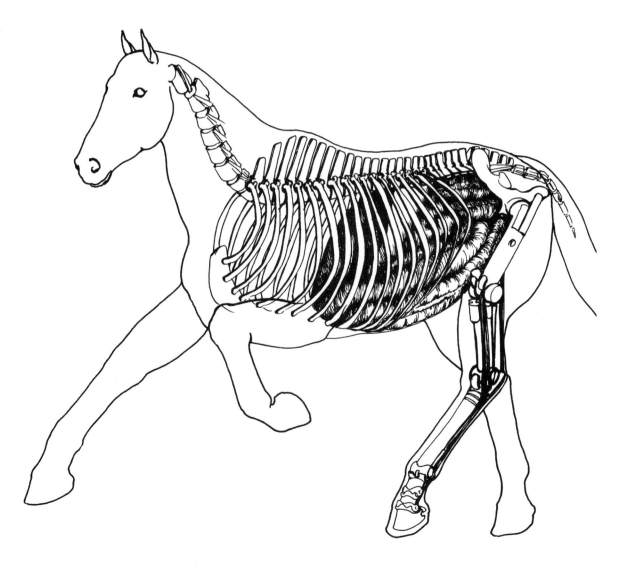

86. He has to lift the contents of the abdomen, even at speed.

87. *Skeletally, the only connection between the hindquarters and the rest of the horse's body is the lumbar spine. The lumbar spine provides areas of attachment for the long back muscles and the back ligaments. These are its only means of support. (The line of the abdomen has been deliberately omitted to make this more apparent.)*

88. Remember the psoas minor and iliopsoas muscles!

1. Psoas minor muscle.
2. Iliopsoas muscle.

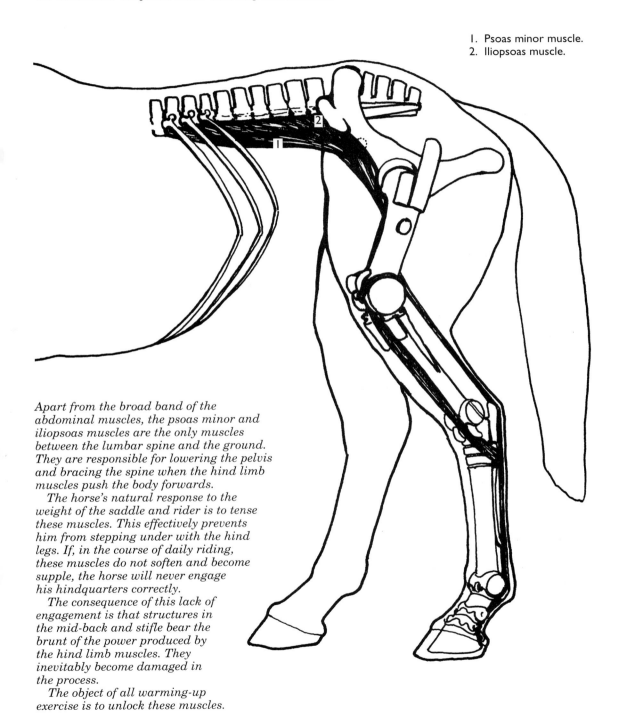

Apart from the broad band of the abdominal muscles, the psoas minor and iliopsoas muscles are the only muscles between the lumbar spine and the ground. They are responsible for lowering the pelvis and bracing the spine when the hind limb muscles push the body forwards.

The horse's natural response to the weight of the saddle and rider is to tense these muscles. This effectively prevents him from stepping under with the hind legs. If, in the course of daily riding, these muscles do not soften and become supple, the horse will never engage his hindquarters correctly.

The consequence of this lack of engagement is that structures in the mid-back and stifle bear the brunt of the power produced by the hind limb muscles. They inevitably become damaged in the process.

The object of all warming-up exercise is to unlock these muscles.

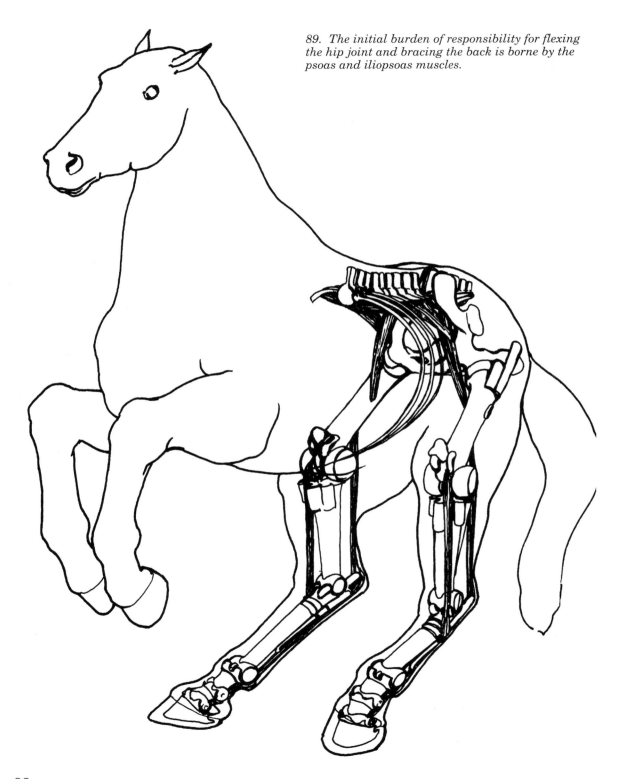

89. *The initial burden of responsibility for flexing the hip joint and bracing the back is borne by the psoas and iliopsoas muscles.*

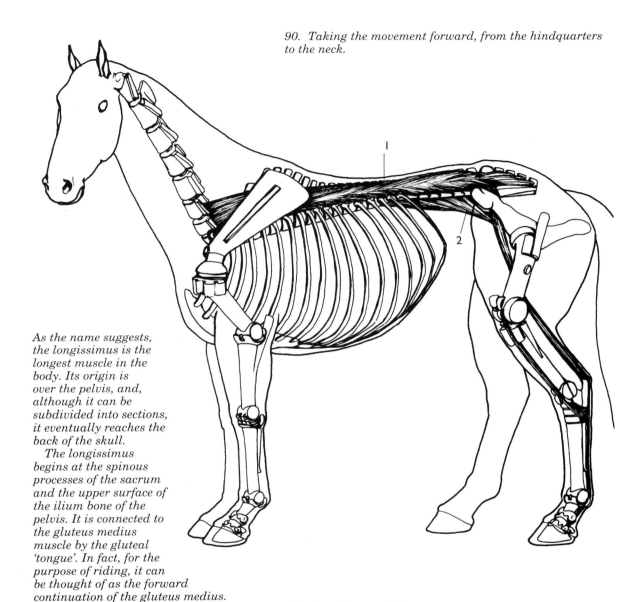

90. *Taking the movement forward, from the hindquarters to the neck.*

As the name suggests, the longissimus is the longest muscle in the body. Its origin is over the pelvis, and, although it can be subdivided into sections, it eventually reaches the back of the skull.

The longissimus begins at the spinous processes of the sacrum and the upper surface of the ilium bone of the pelvis. It is connected to the gluteus medius muscle by the gluteal 'tongue'. In fact, for the purpose of riding, it can be thought of as the forward continuation of the gluteus medius.

The longissimus muscle makes its way towards the withers, picking up small bundles of reinforcing fibres from the dorsal spinous processes of the lumbar and rear thoracic vertebrae. It also forms attachments to each of the transverse processes of the lumbar and thoracic vertebrae and to the tops of the ribs. The thoracic part of the longissimus muscle passes under the scapula and ends at the transverse processes of the last neck bone.

The action of this part of the longissimus muscle is to stabilize the spine during movement, allowing the limbs to swing seamlessly through the phases of protraction and retraction. It goes without saying that, under the rider, this stability should be strong but supple. Any hint of suppleness is lost if, under the lumbar spine, the psoas muscles act as a rigid tow bar.

1. Longissimus muscle (lumbar and thoracic parts).
2. Psoas minor and iliopsis muscles.

99

91. Taking the movement forward, from the hindquarters to the poll.

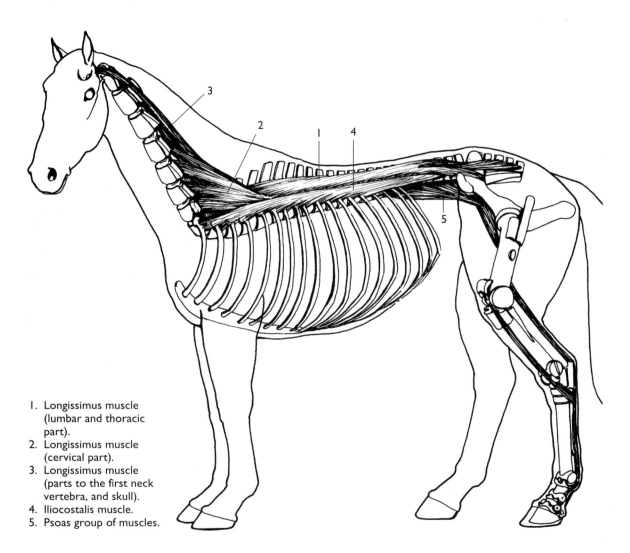

1. Longissimus muscle (lumbar and thoracic part).
2. Longissimus muscle (cervical part).
3. Longissimus muscle (parts to the first neck vertebra, and skull).
4. Iliocostalis muscle.
5. Psoas group of muscles.

The thoracic part of the longissimus muscle ends at the sixth neck vertebra. The neck or cervical part of the longissimus muscle begins at the transverse processes of the last six thoracic vertebrae and fans out to attach to the transverse processes of the neck bones. Two long extensions extend from the vertebrae above the first two ribs to the wing of the atlas (first neck bone), and to the mastoid process of the skull.

The neck portion of the longissimus muscle raises the head and hollows the neck.

The iliocostalis muscle starts over the transverse processes of the lumbar vertebrae. It lies parallel to the longissimus muscle, attaches to the tops of the ribs, and ends at the sixth neck bone. This muscle is used to support the longissimus: it should never be used instead of it.

92. Taking the movement forward: from the back of the neck.

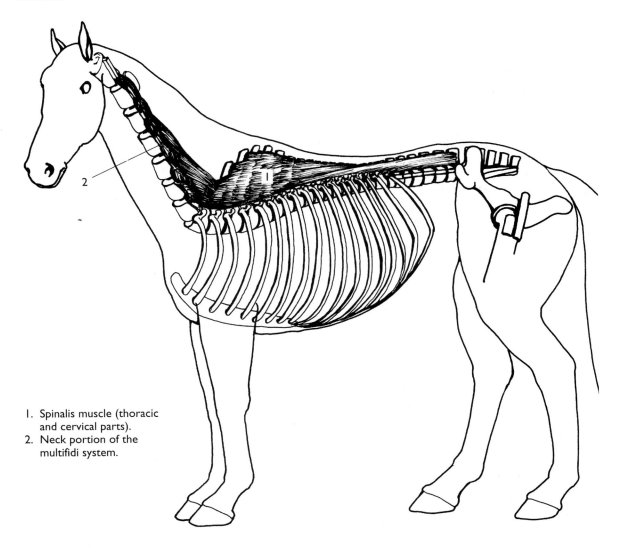

1. Spinalis muscle (thoracic and cervical parts).
2. Neck portion of the multifidi system.

The longissimus muscle has become very familiar – notorious even – owing to the interest of riders in back problems. However, there is a significant muscle that lies between the longissimus and the spinous processes and that is automatically implicated in any painful back.

The spinalis muscle begins at the spinous processes of the lumbar vertebrae. The muscle broadens substantially at the withers and attaches here to the long dorsal spinous processes. From the withers it extends to the third neck vertebra and lies immediately next to the laminae of the nuchal ligament. It inserts on the neck bones between the multifidi muscles.

The spinalis muscle stabilizes the back and lifts the neck.

*93. Taking the movement forward: from the back to
the neck.*

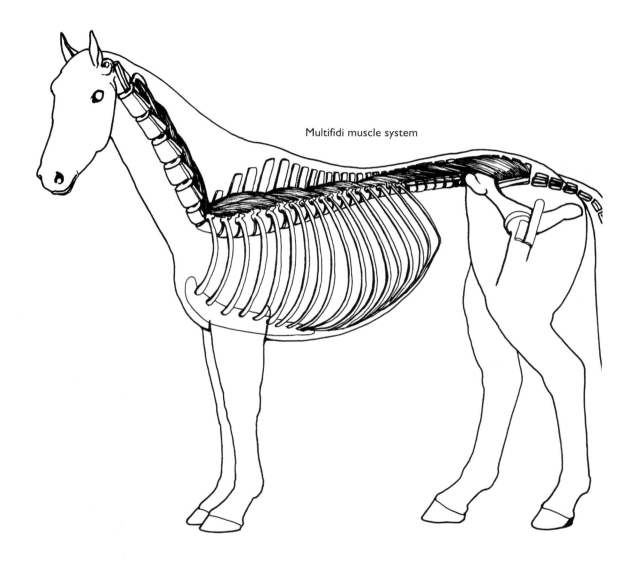

Multifidi muscle system

*The multifidi muscles begin over the sacrum and lumbar vertebrae, connect the dorsal
spinous processes either at their bases or sides, and extend as far forward as the second neck
vertebrae. Like the spinalis and longissimus muscles, the multifidi system is subdivided into
two parts, a thoracic portion and a cervical portion. The junction lies at the base of the neck
in the area of the first rib.*
　The multifidi muscles are primarily stabilizers.

94. *Taking the movement forward: from the*
hindquarters to the poll.

1. Reciprocal apparatus of the hind limb.
2. Psoas muscles.
3. Longissimus muscle (lumbar and
   thoracic parts).
4. Longissimus muscle (cervical part).
5. Longissimus capitis muscle.
6. Longissimus atlantis.
7. Spinalis muscle.
8. Multifidi muscle system (cervical part).
9. Iliocostalis muscle.

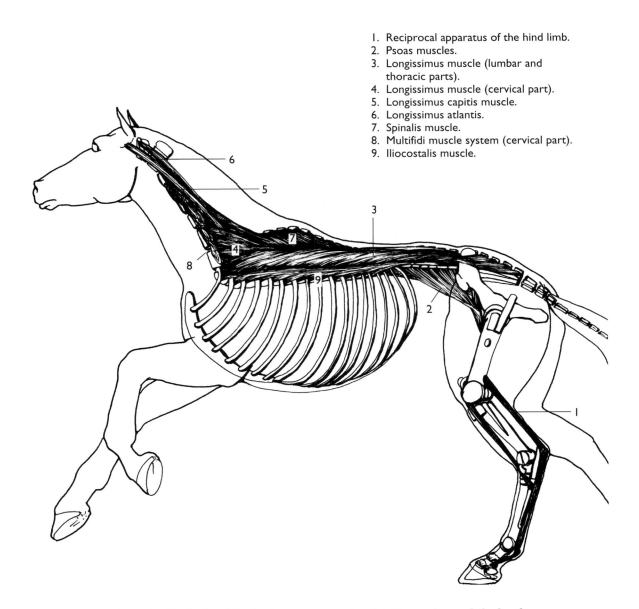

As the horse pushes off with the hind limb, the psoas muscles stabilize and round the lumbar
spine. Then the back muscles extend the spine and raise the head and neck. This lifts the
forehand off the ground. This is the natural mechanism. It is not necessarily appropriate to
all movements when the horse is ridden.

95. *Taking the movement backwards: from the neck to the hind feet.*

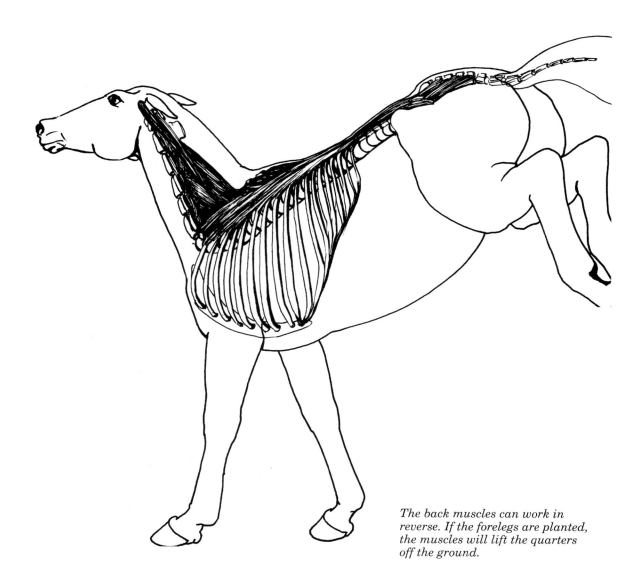

The back muscles can work in reverse. If the forelegs are planted, the muscles will lift the quarters off the ground.

96. The first rib.

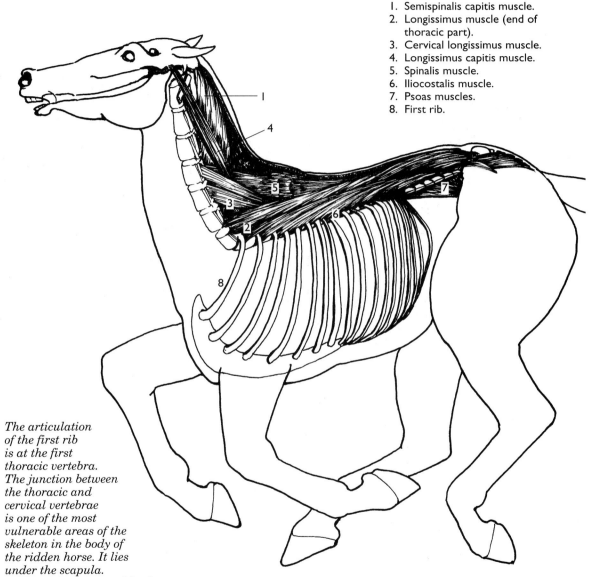

1. Semispinalis capitis muscle.
2. Longissimus muscle (end of thoracic part).
3. Cervical longissimus muscle.
4. Longissimus capitis muscle.
5. Spinalis muscle.
6. Iliocostalis muscle.
7. Psoas muscles.
8. First rib.

The articulation of the first rib is at the first thoracic vertebra. The junction between the thoracic and cervical vertebrae is one of the most vulnerable areas of the skeleton in the body of the ridden horse. It lies under the scapula.

The entire system of back muscles is divided into two major portions. One spans the lumbar and thoracic spine, the other spans the vertebrae of the neck. They all cross over in the region of the first rib.

When maximum force is applied, the back and neck muscles are capable of hyperextending the spine, usually with severe consequences for the structures at the base of the neck. These structures also include nerves.

N.B. The semispinalis capitis muscle is included in this picture. It begins in the fascia underneath the withers, and inserts with a powerful tendon at the back of the skull.

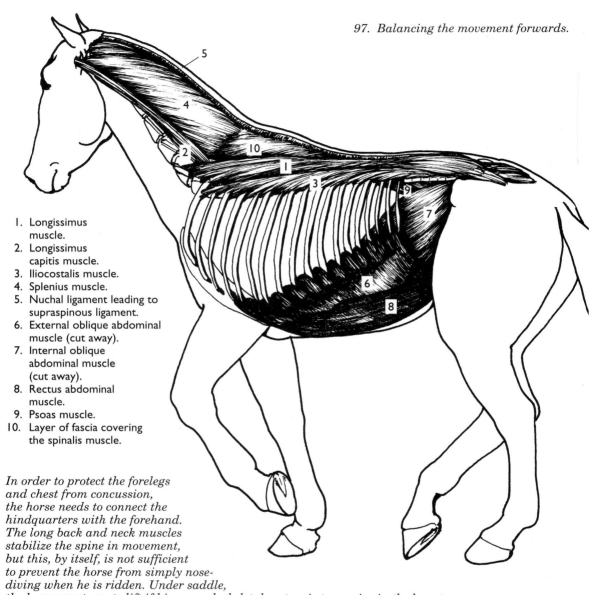

97. Balancing the movement forwards.

1. Longissimus muscle.
2. Longissimus capitis muscle.
3. Iliocostalis muscle.
4. Splenius muscle.
5. Nuchal ligament leading to supraspinous ligament.
6. External oblique abdominal muscle (cut away).
7. Internal oblique abdominal muscle (cut away).
8. Rectus abdominal muscle.
9. Psoas muscle.
10. Layer of fascia covering the spinalis muscle.

In order to protect the forelegs and chest from concussion, the horse needs to connect the hindquarters with the forehand. The long back and neck muscles stabilize the spine in movement, but this, by itself, is not sufficient to prevent the horse from simply nose-diving when he is ridden. Under saddle, the horse must create lift if his musculoskeletal system is to survive in the long term.

The action of the longissimus, iliocostalis and spinalis (not visible here) muscles is to extend the spine: that is, they actually hollow the back and neck. This is because these muscles attach to the upper sides of the vertebrae. When they contract, they pull the spinous processes closer together.

The effect is relatively small between adjacent vertebrae, but it is cumulative over the length of the whole spine. If the horse is unencumbered by the weight of a rider, this extension is good enough to help him 'jump' into the next stride.

In order to sustain elevated movements, and this includes all movements that involve carrying a rider, the horse must be able not only to brace his back, but also to strengthen it. The momentum from the hind limb muscles has to be channelled back to the quarters, otherwise there is an unnecessary expenditure of energy.

The splenius muscle is a balancing muscle. For example, when the horse is galloping, this muscle creates the characteristic neck movements. The splenius begins in fascia at the withers (under the scapula), and also attaches to the nuchal ligament. It inserts on the transverse processes of the third, fourth and fifth neck vertebrae. But, most significantly, it joins the brachiocephalicus and longissimus capitis muscles at their insertions on the skull. The splenius muscle mediates between the angle of the head, traction of the nuchal ligament, forward reach of the forelimb, and position of the neck bones. In other words, the splenius muscle is the barometer of self-carriage.

However, we are still left with that most vulnerable of places, the junction of the thoracic and cervical spine under the articulating head of the first rib. It is vital that the strengthening action of the muscles embraces this junction, and it is for this very reason that the two systems of back and neck muscles overlap. Nature knows that this is an area of high risk.

The action of the back and neck muscles must pass seamlessly from chest to neck. But it can only do this if the horse uses the abdominal muscles. Remember the bow and bowstring effect. When the abdominal muscles tighten, they apply traction to the lumbar and rear thoracic spine. When the long back muscles attempt to extend the spine, they pull not on the spinous processes but against the abdominal muscles. The top and bottom lines of the horse's body become united in a closed curve, which, like the oval shape of a rugby ball, allows the horse to bounce onwards and, most importantly, upwards.

98. Pulling the head and neck down.

1. Sternomandibularis muscle.
2. Sternohyoideus muscle.
3. Longus colli muscles.
4. Tongue.

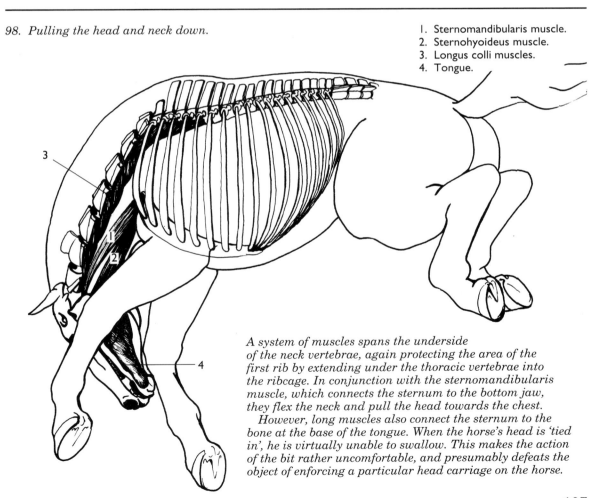

A system of muscles spans the underside of the neck vertebrae, again protecting the area of the first rib by extending under the thoracic vertebrae into the ribcage. In conjunction with the sternomandibularis muscle, which connects the sternum to the bottom jaw, they flex the neck and pull the head towards the chest.

However, long muscles also connect the sternum to the bone at the base of the tongue. When the horse's head is 'tied in', he is virtually unable to swallow. This makes the action of the bit rather uncomfortable, and presumably defeats the object of enforcing a particular head carriage on the horse.

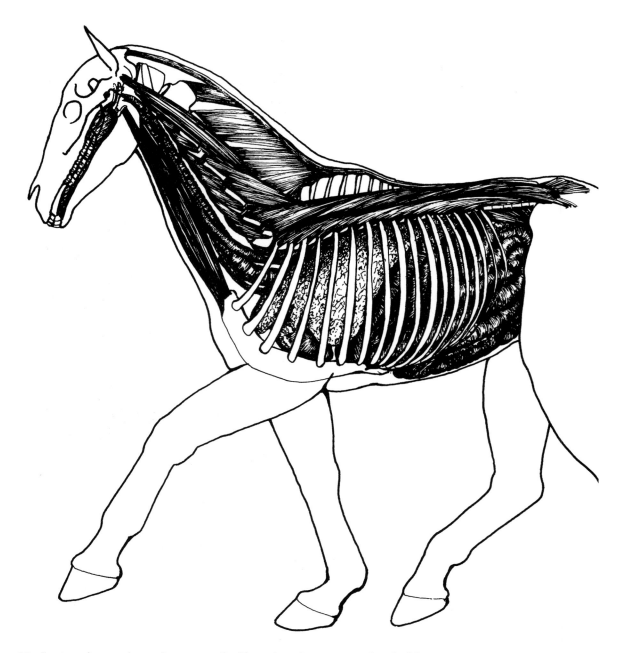

99. *Lest we forget: the real purpose of self-carriage is to protect the vital inner organs.*

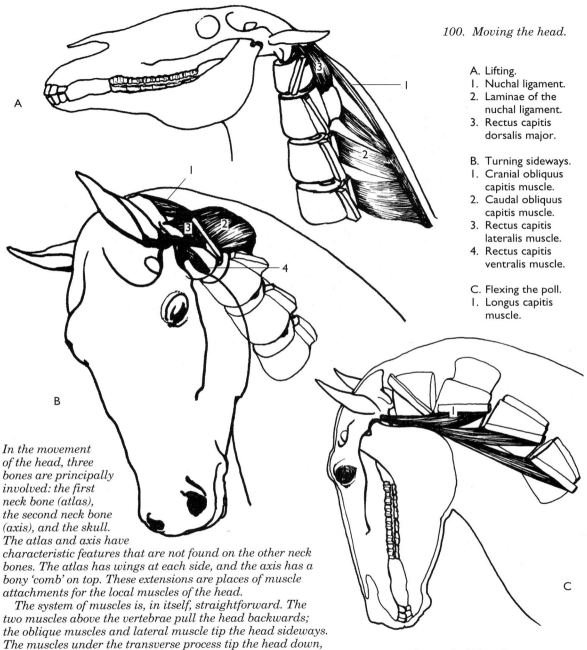

100. Moving the head.

A. Lifting.
1. Nuchal ligament.
2. Laminae of the nuchal ligament.
3. Rectus capitis dorsalis major.

B. Turning sideways.
1. Cranial obliquus capitis muscle.
2. Caudal obliquus capitis muscle.
3. Rectus capitis lateralis muscle.
4. Rectus capitis ventralis muscle.

C. Flexing the poll.
1. Longus capitis muscle.

In the movement of the head, three bones are principally involved: the first neck bone (atlas), the second neck bone (axis), and the skull. The atlas and axis have characteristic features that are not found on the other neck bones. The atlas has wings at each side, and the axis has a bony 'comb' on top. These extensions are places of muscle attachments for the local muscles of the head.

The system of muscles is, in itself, straightforward. The two muscles above the vertebrae pull the head backwards; the oblique muscles and lateral muscle tip the head sideways. The muscles under the transverse process tip the head down, flexing the poll. The significance of these muscles is that they are prone to tension and subjected to one-sided use. The joint between the atlas and the skull is a pivotal point in the horse's system of balance. If the horse has to tip his head to keep his balance, or the rider is uneven with the aids (particularly with that less sympathetic left hand), the effects will be concentrated at the poll.

These small muscles are a major source of headaches, in more ways than one!

N.B. When the head is tipped backwards, the nuchal ligament is slackened. This reduces its traction on the laminae and the supraspinous ligament.

109

101. Moving the jaw.

1. Masseter muscle.
2. Pterygoideus muscle.
3. Temporalis muscle.
4. Digastricus muscle.
5. Pulling the jaw sideways: the masseter muscle.

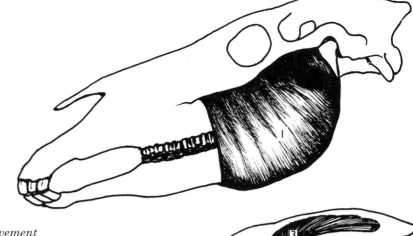

The principal direction of movement in the horse's lower jaw is from side to side. This enables the premolar and molar teeth to grind plant material, which constitutes much of the horse's natural diet.

The sizeable masseter muscles on the outside of the jawbones can work both simultaneously and alternately. They either press the teeth together, or move the lower teeth sideways. The masseter is assisted by the pterygoideus muscle on the inside of the jaw.

A double-bellied muscle called the digastricus attaches the lower jaw to the base of the skull. It pulls the jaw backwards. The temporalis muscle acts on the lever-like extension of the jawbone above the eye socket, pressing the lower teeth against those in the upper jaw.

The upper jaw is wider than the lower jaw. When the upper back teeth develop sharp edges, the masseter muscle is braced to prevent these points from lacerating the gums. This not only affects the application of the bit, it also interferes with the action of those neck muscles that attach directly behind the jaw to the mastoid process of the skull: the brachiocephalicus, longissimus capitis and splenius muscles.

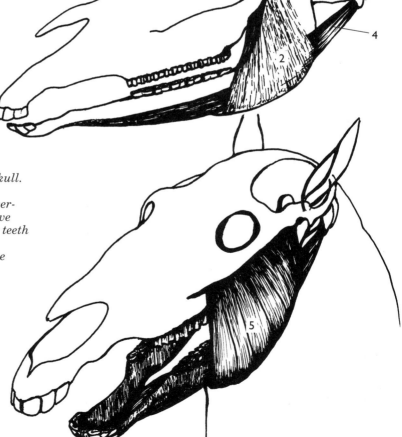

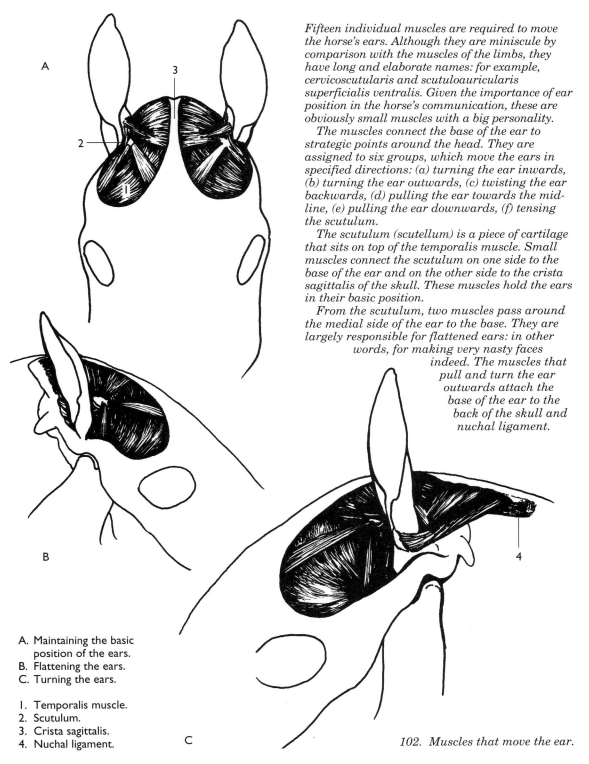

Fifteen individual muscles are required to move the horse's ears. Although they are miniscule by comparison with the muscles of the limbs, they have long and elaborate names: for example, cervicoscutularis and scutuloauricularis superficialis ventralis. Given the importance of ear position in the horse's communication, these are obviously small muscles with a big personality.

The muscles connect the base of the ear to strategic points around the head. They are assigned to six groups, which move the ears in specified directions: (a) turning the ear inwards, (b) turning the ear outwards, (c) twisting the ear backwards, (d) pulling the ear towards the mid-line, (e) pulling the ear downwards, (f) tensing the scutulum.

The scutulum (scutellum) is a piece of cartilage that sits on top of the temporalis muscle. Small muscles connect the scutulum on one side to the base of the ear and on the other side to the crista sagittalis of the skull. These muscles hold the ears in their basic position.

From the scutulum, two muscles pass around the medial side of the ear to the base. They are largely responsible for flattened ears: in other words, for making very nasty faces indeed. The muscles that pull and turn the ear outwards attach the base of the ear to the back of the skull and nuchal ligament.

A. Maintaining the basic position of the ears.
B. Flattening the ears.
C. Turning the ears.

1. Temporalis muscle.
2. Scutulum.
3. Crista sagittalis.
4. Nuchal ligament.

102. Muscles that move the ear.

111

103. A most particular ear muscle.

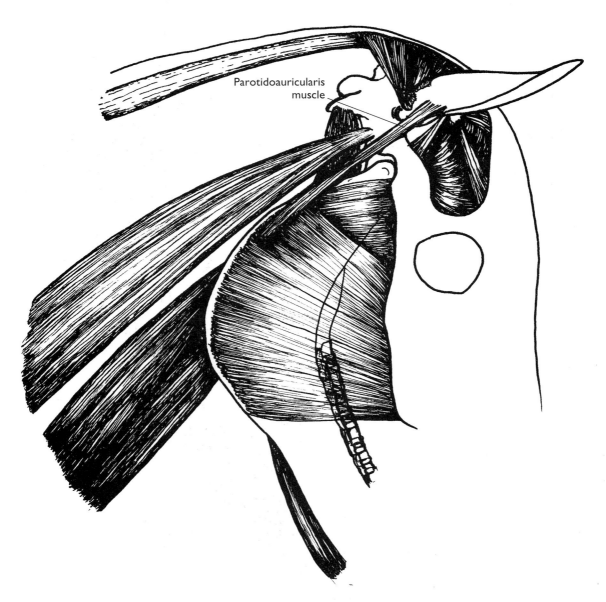

Parotidoauricularis
muscle

Horses do not disguise their emotions. Their ears give them away. Obviously, since the ears can be moved by any of fifteen different muscles, the emotional language is not without subtlety. However, there is one muscle that should speak to us above all others: the one responsible for pulling the ear downwards, the parotidoauricularis muscle.

If there is any restriction around the area of the jaw, caused by a hard hand, inaccurate aids, imbalance of the atlas, riding the horse on the forehand, sharp teeth, tying the horse's head in, poorly fitting bridle (the list could go on), the tension will be reflected in this muscle. In a horse that is going softly, the ears will move passively to the rhythm of the head and neck.

1. Orbicularis oris, a ring of muscle, closes the mouth.
2. Levator nasolabialis raises the upper lip, dilates the nostril, and sometimes produces worry lines.
3. Levator labii maxillaris raises the upper lip.
4. Caninus dilates the nostril.
5. Zygomaticus draws back the corners of the mouth.
6. Buccinator brings the food from the gums to the back teeth.
7. Dilator naris apicalis dilates the nostril.
8. Orbicularis oculi, a ring of muscle, closes the eyelids.
9. Levator anguli oculi raises the upper eyelid.
10. Malaris pulls the lower eyelid down.

N.B. The muscles that pull down the lower lip are not shown in this view.

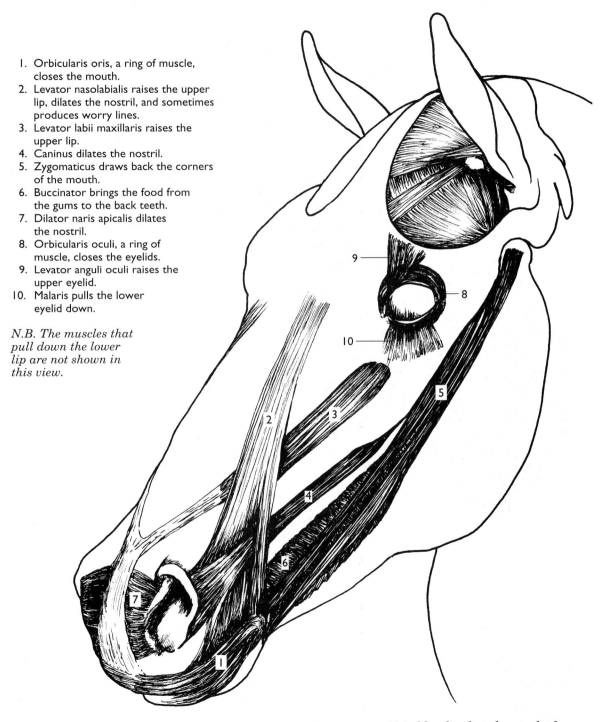

104. Muscles that change the face.

105. Last, but by no means least: muscles that move the tail.

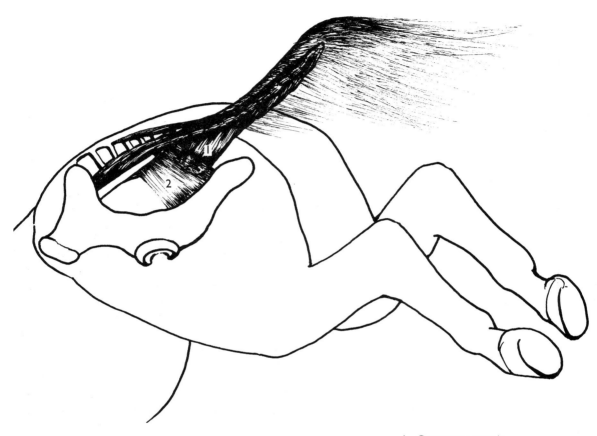

1. Coccygeus muscle.
2. Sacrotuberal ligament.

There are, in fact, four systems of muscle that move the tail. They are continuations of the longissimus and multifidi muscles of the back, and insert along the spinous processes of the tail vertebrae, along the transverse processes, and underneath the vertebral bodies. They therefore pull the tail upwards, sideways, and downwards.

The coccygeus muscle attaches under the broad sacrotuberal ligament and inserts on the transverse processes of the first four tail vertebrae. This muscle clamps the tail down.

N.B. Like all the muscles of the neck and back, the tail muscles can be used on one side of the body only. In the case of the back muscles, one-sided use produces bend. In the case of the tail muscles, it produces swish.

4 The Wiring: Nerves

One characteristic makes the horse more suited to riding than any other species – his fundamental obedience. To be sure, the horse's back looks inviting and virtually demands to be sat on. Yet there are plenty of animals whose backs are stronger and more stable, and whose paces are smoother and less prone to fluctuations of rhythm. Nevertheless, horses are ridden the world over, which suggests that there may be more to the point of riding than simply the convenience of getting from A to B.

The casual expression, 'a push-button ride' – summing up the rideability of a horse – is not always a compliment, since it does not tell us whether the horse is obedient because he has been well educated, or obedient because he has been thoroughly conditioned. Nevertheless, the concept of pushing buttons, even if they are the wrong ones, encapsulates the idea that riding horses has something to do with activating quick-firing electrical circuits that, in turn, produce a series of reliable mechanical responses.

In technology, push-buttons are small round objects that operate electrical devices. It can be misleading to use images associated with inanimate objects to describe the physiological behaviour of living beings. Such comparisons are often simplistic. However, although the surface of the horse's body is not literally strewn with hundreds of plastic knobs, it is certainly wired to a wide range of electrical equipment, all of which triggers some sort of activity in the horse's musculoskeletal system.

Without electricity, no horse, or human, would be able to move. Electricity is produced by the positive and negative charges of the body's chemicals. Small electrical currents flow across the cell membranes, provoking palpable reactions in certain types of tissue. For example, when electrolytes change places in the compartments of muscle cells, the muscle fibres are stimulated to contract.

If the contractions of muscles are to be meaningful, they have to be supervised and coordinated. The muscles, like a corps de ballet, need directing, so that the raising and lowering of a leg (or a neck, or back) is carried out as a sequence of graceful gestures, not a series of disproportionate jerks. Choreographer-in-chief is the brain, although its role is more like one of general artistic director. The brain creates the ideas; the ideas are made into reality by nerves. Like 'repetiteurs' in a rehearsal room, the nerves instruct the muscles on how to perform the movements.

All movement is a process of constant rehearsal. The muscles have to repeat sequences of movement until they have grasped the routine. Once the routine is refined, it is stored, and then recalled as part of an established movement repertoire.

As riders, we are inclined to take the movement of the horse for granted. Despite current trends in rider awareness, despite the provision of information on equine lameness, despite the accessibility of chiropractors and physiotherapists, we still regularly fail to see the most basic connection: that when we ride horses, we become the chief choreographers. The nerves instruct the muscles according to our understanding of the dance.

Under the influence of a rider, a horse's movements are never the same as when he is unridden. They may come very close, and the free paces may be used by a skilled rider to his advantage. Nevertheless, the presence of a rider, together with that of the saddle and bridle, always impinges on the horse's musculoskeletal system. It must do because it is foreign to the horse's body. Consequently, when we sit on the horse's back, we change the natural parameters of the horse's movement. We expand his frame to incorporate our own. It is therefore part of the art of riding to ensure that this expansion does not create areas of weakness. For we choose to ride horses not because their backs are stronger than those of other animals, but because they are infinitely more flexible.

For example, if you watch young cattle trotting down the slope of a field, you will notice that not only do they spontaneously lengthen their strides, they automatically suspend their backs. The horizontal profile of the cow's back gives it considerable stability, and it does not take much in the way of muscle power to sustain this. The construction of the horse's back is altogether less rigid than that of the cow. However, its shape gives it greater versatility. The topline is more rounded, the quarters more sloping, the contours of the withers are more pronounced and purposeful. The whole profile is elevated by the sweeping curve of the neck. This is a body with upward mobility. But at what cost?

When the horse trots down a slope, he, too, can lengthen his stride. He can, if he chooses, also stabilize his back. But he is more likely, in the first instance, to balance his body simply by using the neck muscles. The next 'string to his bow' is to lift the suspension around the chest, and then tighten the support of the abdomen. This increases the traction along the back ligaments. Only when these measures fail to protect the body from jarring does it become necessary for the horse to brace his back using the long back muscles. In most free-moving situations, the horse can bounce along quite happily without them.

In the unridden horse, the use of the long back muscles, like that of the abdominal muscles, is not an essential part of reducing concussion on the body. The body muscles are deployed as the situation arises. However, this is not true of horses that are ridden. Here the contribution of the back and abdominal muscles is vital. The use of these muscles means the difference between soft paces and stiff paces, between a horse that lifts the rider into each stride and one that hangs like a dead weight on the rider's arms, between a horse that carries himself with lightness, and one that runs along on the forehand. In fact, the muscular support of the spine and abdomen is the key to the success of the whole riding operation.

Nevertheless, the horse cannot be relied on to implement these muscles just because we put him under saddle. As far as he is concerned, they are not always appropriate, and, more importantly, their use costs him a great deal of extra effort. It is up to the rider to ask for this stability because, ultimately, it is in his and the horse's best interest. How does the rider ask? Well, to begin with, he has to learn about the push-buttons.

Knowing the location of the horse's muscles is one thing, but knowing how to make these muscles work for us is quite another. We need to remind ourselves that although it is the horse's muscles that carry us around the arena, it is the horse's nerves that put us in the privileged position of command. In other words, when we sit deep in the saddle, squeeze with the calf muscles, square the shoulders, lift the chest, drive with the seat bones, and look straight between the horse's ears, we are not just giving the aids for walk, trot or canter. We are, in fact, making a whole series of strategic neurological requests, which reach the muscles in the form of electrical signals along the nerves. It is thanks to the unique sensitivity of these nerves, and their position close to the rider's seat and legs, that we can expect the horse to do what we ask.

Nerves are the electrical equipment that drives the musculoskeletal machine. The instrument panel is spread right across the horse's body. It is our responsibility, as riders, to operate the machine wisely. But we can only do this if we know how to push the right buttons.

106. A single nerve cell.

1. Cell body.
2. Dendrite.
3. Axon.
4. Neuromuscular
   endplate.

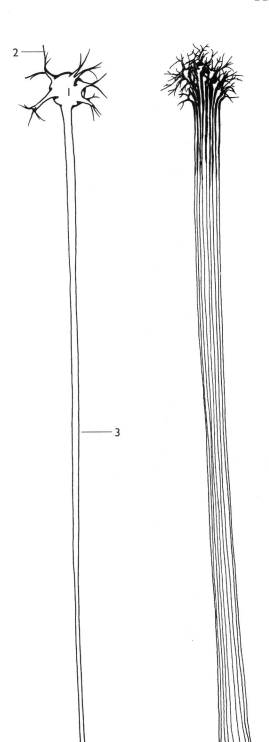

Nerve cells come in a variety of shapes. But whether they belong to the central nervous system and are located in the brain, or belong to the peripheral nervous system and are found in the spinal cord, they are all constructed along similar lines. They fulfil the same basic function, which is to receive and transmit information in the form of small electrical signals.

The nerve cell has two types of extension. The short-branched extensions (dendrites) around the cell body receive information from other nerve cells. The long, single extension (axon) is the transmitter. In the musculoskeletal system, nerves of the type shown here (motor nerves) transmit signals to activate the muscles.

The remarkable thing about motor nerves is that if, for example, the body of this cell was on the first page of this book, the axon would be long enough to follow the folds of each page until it reached this page. Yet the impulses travel from the nerve cell to the muscle in milliseconds.

Just as one skeletal muscle comprises many bundles of fibres, one nerve consists of the extensions of many nerve cells. Like the muscle fibres, these nerve fibres are wrapped together in small groups, and then bound into larger bundles.

It is important to realize that the bundles of fibres, which constitute the individual nerves, are not microscopic filaments, nor do they transmit their signals through the ether. They have very tangible thickness and substance (which, in the case of the sciatic nerve, is quite considerable). They are capable of being squashed, shredded or torn, just like the cable of any electrical appliance.

107. A single nerve.

108. The spinal cord: a chain of command.

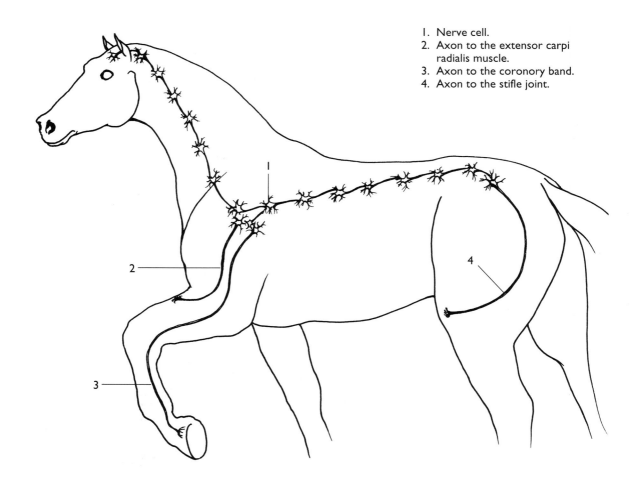

1. Nerve cell.
2. Axon to the extensor carpi radialis muscle.
3. Axon to the coronory band.
4. Axon to the stifle joint.

The spinal cord is a chain of nerve cells. (Here, only a series of individual cells is shown. In reality, there are of course many hundreds.) The spinal cord passes instructions from the brain to the muscles.

The diagram shows how the length of axons varies according to their destination in the horse's body.

118

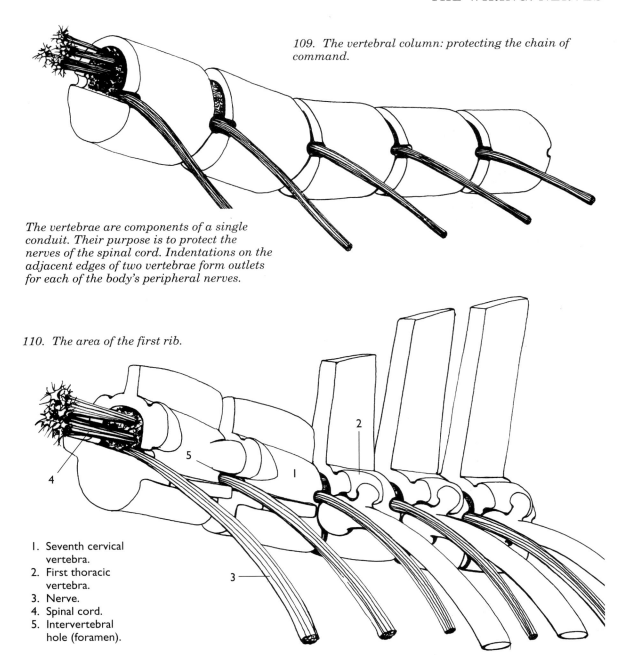

109. The vertebral column: protecting the chain of command.

The vertebrae are components of a single conduit. Their purpose is to protect the nerves of the spinal cord. Indentations on the adjacent edges of two vertebrae form outlets for each of the body's peripheral nerves.

110. The area of the first rib.

1. Seventh cervical
   vertebra.
2. First thoracic
   vertebra.
3. Nerve.
4. Spinal cord.
5. Intervertebral
   hole (foramen).

The fibres that make up each peripheral nerve leave the relative safety of the spinal cord through the intervertebral holes. This happens along the entire length of the spine as far as the sacrum.

In the region of the ribs, the nerves have to bypass the double articulations of the rib heads (here exaggerated). Although the construction of the upper chest is stabilized by ligaments and several overlapping systems of muscles, there is absolutely no room for unwanted tension. It is bound to make the tissues impinge on the nerves.

119

111. The area of the first rib.

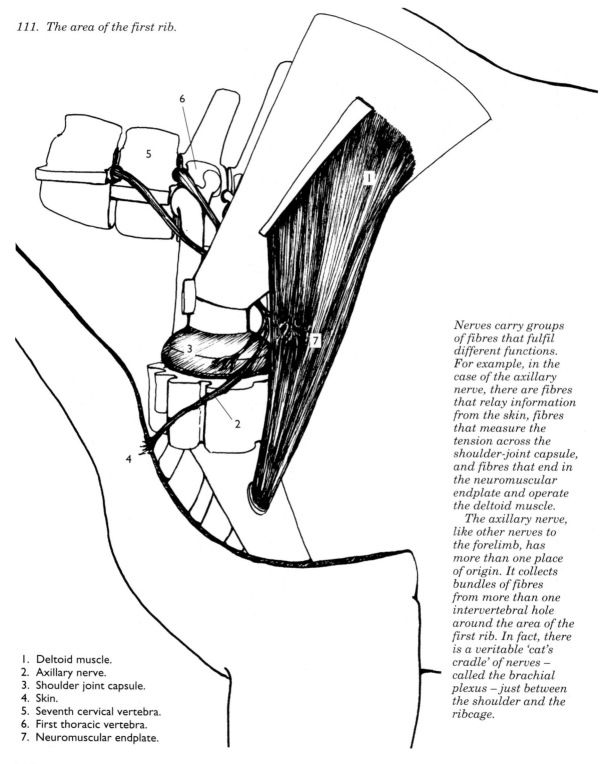

Nerves carry groups
of fibres that fulfil
different functions.
For example, in the
case of the axillary
nerve, there are fibres
that relay information
from the skin, fibres
that measure the
tension across the
shoulder-joint capsule,
and fibres that end in
the neuromuscular
endplate and operate
the deltoid muscle.

The axillary nerve,
like other nerves to
the forelimb, has
more than one place
of origin. It collects
bundles of fibres
from more than one
intervertebral hole
around the area of the
first rib. In fact, there
is a veritable 'cat's
cradle' of nerves –
called the brachial
plexus – just between
the shoulder and the
ribcage.

1. Deltoid muscle.
2. Axillary nerve.
3. Shoulder joint capsule.
4. Skin.
5. Seventh cervical vertebra.
6. First thoracic vertebra.
7. Neuromuscular endplate.

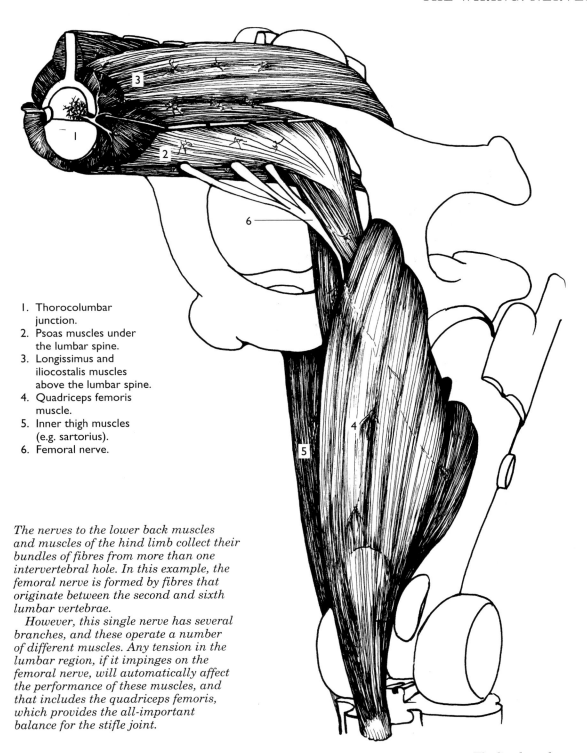

1. Thorocolumbar junction.
2. Psoas muscles under the lumbar spine.
3. Longissimus and iliocostalis muscles above the lumbar spine.
4. Quadriceps femoris muscle.
5. Inner thigh muscles (e.g. sartorius).
6. Femoral nerve.

The nerves to the lower back muscles and muscles of the hind limb collect their bundles of fibres from more than one intervertebral hole. In this example, the femoral nerve is formed by fibres that originate between the second and sixth lumbar vertebrae.

However, this single nerve has several branches, and these operate a number of different muscles. Any tension in the lumbar region, if it impinges on the femoral nerve, will automatically affect the performance of these muscles, and that includes the quadriceps femoris, which provides the all-important balance for the stifle joint.

112. The lumbar plexus.

113. The area under the saddle.

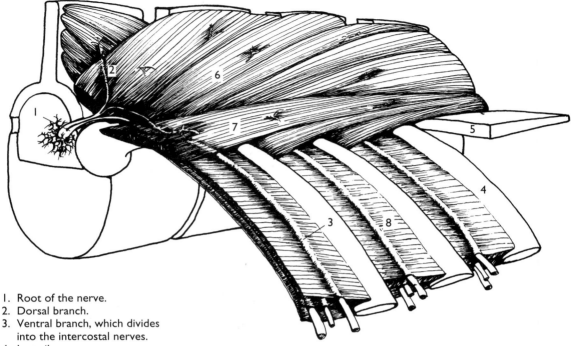

1. Root of the nerve.
2. Dorsal branch.
3. Ventral branch, which divides into the intercostal nerves.
4. Last rib.
5. Transverse process of the first lumbar vertebra.
6. Longissimus muscle.
7. Iliocostalis muscle.
8. External intercostal muscle.

Each nerve, as it leaves the spinal canal, divides into an upper (dorsal) and lower (ventral) branch. The dorsal branches operate the muscles that lie above the spine; the ventral branches operate the muscles that lie below, or to the side of, the spine. This system, with few exceptions, is true for the whole length of the spinal column.

The dorsal and ventral branches each divide again into thinner branches that operate different tiers of muscles. In the case of the thoracic nerves, there are three, extensive branches that pass between the layers of the intercostal muscles, and also between these muscles and the pleural lining of the chest cavity.

There is only one thing that separates these nerves and nerve-endings from direct contact with the saddle and the rider's boots, and that is the horse's skin. There is nothing else. Whatever we do with our legs and seat, the effect is fairly immediate.

The ventral and dorsal branches are connected, which means that wherever we apply the pressure of the legs, this place communicates with the same specific segment of the horse's back muscles. However, nerves work by transmitting intermittent impulses: constant or substantial pressure actually switches them off. Therefore, if we clamp the legs around the horse's ribcage in an effort to 'drive' him forwards, it is certainly as counter-productive as ramming the seat bones down into the saddle. The effect is, quite literally, numbing.

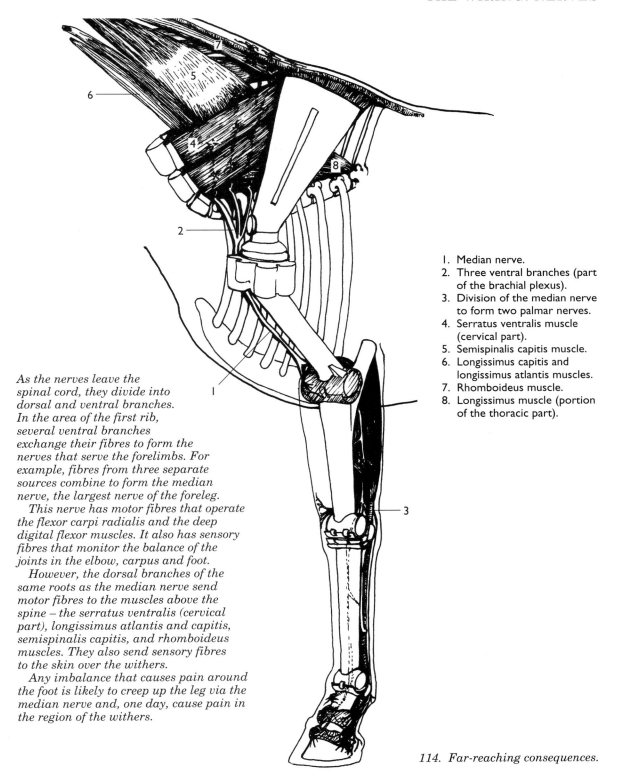

1. Median nerve.
2. Three ventral branches (part of the brachial plexus).
3. Division of the median nerve to form two palmar nerves.
4. Serratus ventralis muscle (cervical part).
5. Semispinalis capitis muscle.
6. Longissimus capitis and longissimus atlantis muscles.
7. Rhomboideus muscle.
8. Longissimus muscle (portion of the thoracic part).

As the nerves leave the spinal cord, they divide into dorsal and ventral branches. In the area of the first rib, several ventral branches exchange their fibres to form the nerves that serve the forelimbs. For example, fibres from three separate sources combine to form the median nerve, the largest nerve of the foreleg.

This nerve has motor fibres that operate the flexor carpi radialis and the deep digital flexor muscles. It also has sensory fibres that monitor the balance of the joints in the elbow, carpus and foot.

However, the dorsal branches of the same roots as the median nerve send motor fibres to the muscles above the spine – the serratus ventralis (cervical part), longissimus atlantis and capitis, semispinalis capitis, and rhomboideus muscles. They also send sensory fibres to the skin over the withers.

Any imbalance that causes pain around the foot is likely to creep up the leg via the median nerve and, one day, cause pain in the region of the withers.

114. Far-reaching consequences.

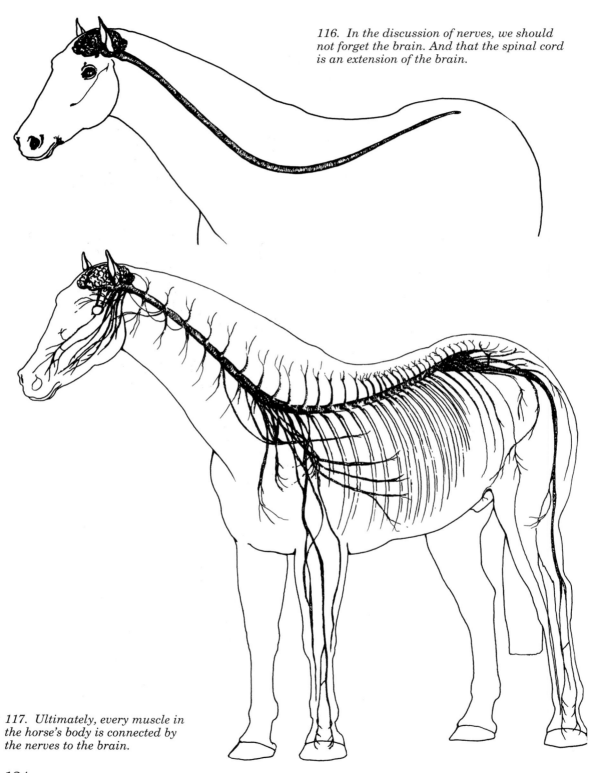

116. *In the discussion of nerves, we should not forget the brain. And that the spinal cord is an extension of the brain.*

117. *Ultimately, every muscle in the horse's body is connected by the nerves to the brain.*

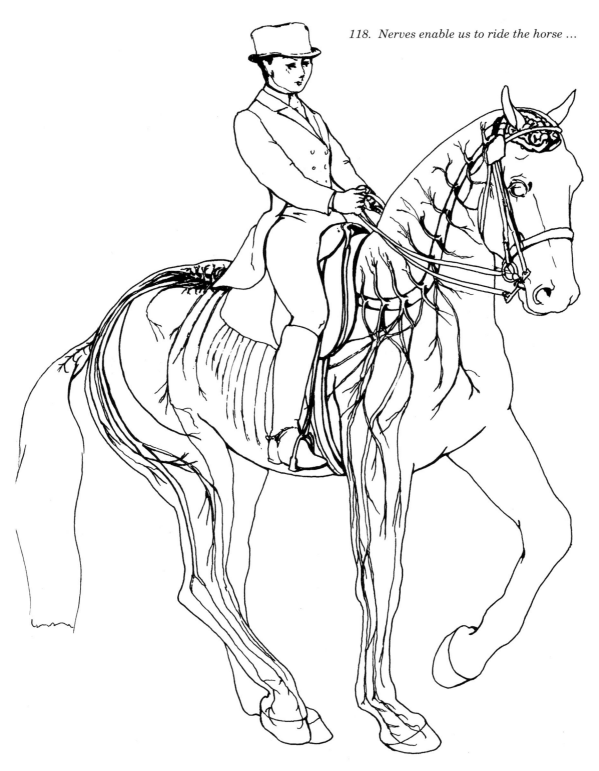

118. Nerves enable us to ride the horse ...

119. ... the muscles just help us to win.

Postscript ————————————————————————

The last novel by the famous Russian author, Fyodor Dostoyevsky, is usually known as *The Brothers Karamazov*. However, a present-day translator recently decided to change the title, calling it instead *The Karamazov Brothers*. After all, we don't refer to other public figures as the brothers Wright or the twins Kray.

Of course, by altering the word order, the translator removed some of the original title's mystique. But by giving the book a plain-speaking title, he opened up the book to readers who might otherwise have thought it too 'literary' or high-brow.

However, whether you prefer your Karamazov before, or after, your Brothers, theirs is a good story, and so, too, is the story of the horse's anatomy. If, by translating it into the form of mechanical prose, this anatomy has lost something of its mystique, we can be sure to find the poetry again just as soon as we look at the horse.

'It seems to me that if one were to recall and explain everything properly, it would fill a whole volume, and a very large one at that. And so I trust that my readers will not complain if I describe only what struck me personally and what stuck in my mind … and that they will realize themselves that I have done all I could.' (Fyodor Dostoyevsky: *The Brothers Karamazov* (1880), Book Twelve, The Fatal Day.)

Index